Edible for the Irritable

COOKBOOK

A Cookbook for Coeliacs and IBS Sufferers

Spencer Clements

Edible for the Irritable
COOKBOOK

A Cookbook for Coeliacs
and IBS Sufferers

Spencer Clements

NEW HOLLAND

Contents

Introduction

Why should everyone else have all the fun? Coeliacs and IBS sufferers want to enjoy eating with their family and friends. This cookbook demonstrates that eating gluten-free food doesn't mean compromising on taste or missing out on the joys of cooking.

I have always had a passion for cooking from the age of ten. Now that I'm in my thirties and have been diagnosed with IBS (irritable bowel syndrome), I want to learn more about it and to help others who have this disease.

Eating in restaurants can be a problem for coeliacs and IBS sufferers, so chefs and restaurant owners can also take a few tips from this book. Taking gluten out of your diet is not a fashion statement—it's a disease and must be treated carefully. Many chefs are often unaware that even just the smallest amount of flour or flour-based products can cause a problem. Flour is air-born and can get into anything so chefs need to take special care in the workplace to prevent cross-contamination.

All the recipes I have developed are simple and uncomplicated. Many are a one pot wonder.

The first step to a great meal is to create a food cupboard that contains all the basic ingredients for your gluten-free cooking. I'm sure once you get started with this book, you will find yourself on a cooking adventure of sweet and savoury foods that you just can't stop making! There are plenty of gluten-free products available these days, but there's nothing better than making your own and saving some money. To make it easier, in most of the recipes I use kitchen aid equipment. These machines will be your friend forever and will make your life so much easier.

Once you get the idea and the hang of the recipe, the sky's the limit.

Problem Foods

Grains/Cereals/Flours

Barley

Legumes (chickpeas, lentils, red kidney beans, baked beans)

Rye (in large amounts; bread, rye crackers)

Wheat (in large amounts; bread, pasta, couscous, crackers, biscuits)

Vegetables

Artichoke

Avocado

Beetroot

Broccoli

Brussels sprout

Cabbage

Cauliflower

Celery

Chick peas

Fennel

Garlic

Green capsicum (peppers)

Leek

Mushroom

Okra

Onion (white, brown, spring, Spanish, shallot, leek)

Peas

Snow peas

Sugar snap peas

Sweet corn

Fruit

Apple

Blackberry

Cherry

Custard apple

Dried fruit

Fructose

High-fructose corn syrup

Longon

Lychee

Mango

Nashi pear

Pear

Persimmon

Plum

Rambutan

Stone fruit (clingstone peach, white peach, apricot, nectarine)

Tinned fruit in natural juice

Watermelon

Sauces/Condiments

Artificially sweetened gum, mint (sorbitol, mannitol, xylitol, isomalt)

Barbecue sauce

Chicory (Ecco, caro, dandelion tea)

Commercial gravy

Commercial stock

Fructo-oligosaccharide (FOS, Fibre in some nutritional supplements)

Garlic powder

Honey

Inulin (fibre in some dairy products)

Onion powder

Tartare sauce

Worcestershire sauce

Dairy

Condensed milk

Cow's milk (regular/low fat)

Custard

Ice cream

Soft cheese (ricotta, cottage)

Yoghurt (regular and low fat)

Safe Foods

Grains/Cereals/Flours

Cornflakes
Cornflour
Gluten-free biscuits
Gluten-free bread
Gluten-free flour
Gluten-free pasta
Muesli (wheat, dairy, nut and fruit-free)
Oat bran
Puffed rice
Rice (white or brown)
Rice noodles

Vegetables

Bamboo shoot
Bean sprouts
Bok choy
Carrot
Celery
Chives
Choko
Choy sum
Corn
Cucumber
Eggplant (aubergine)
Green bean
Lettuce (iceberg or coral)
Olive
Parsnip
Potato
Pumpkin
Red capsicum (bell pepper)
Silverbeet
Spinach (silverbeet)
Spring onion (green part only)
Squash
Tomato
Turnip
Zucchini (courgette)

Fruit

Banana
Grape
Mandarine
Orange
Kiwifruit
Rockmelon (cantaloupe)
Honey dew melon
Pineapple
Carrabolla
Berries (strawberries, raspberries, blueberries)
Tangelo
Paw paw
Rhubarb
Grapefruit
Lemon
Lime
Passionfruit
Durian

Sauces/Condiments

Chilli powder
Herbs (fresh and dry)
Jam
Lemon juice
Mayonnaise
Oil/butter
Oyster sauce
(in moderate amounts)
Pure 100% meat stock
(no onion, no garlic)
Soy sauce
Table sugar

Dairy

Hard cheddar cheese
Lactose-free milk
Lactose-free yoghurt
Rice milk

What is Coeliac Disease?

Coeliac disease (pronounced seel-ee-ak) is an autoimmune disease where the body produces antibodies that damage its own tissues. It is a permanent intestinal intolerance to dietary gluten—a protein found in wheat, rye, barley and oats.

If coeliac disease is not treated, the tiny, finger-like projections (villi) in the lining of the small intestine become damaged and flattened. This is known as villous atrophy. If this occurs, the person's ability to break down and absorb nutrients from food is significantly reduced, leading to numerous vitamin and mineral deficiencies.

Untreated coeliac disease can lead to chronic poor health, osteoporosis, infertility, miscarriage, depression and dental enamel defects. There is also a small, but real, increased risk of certain forms of cancer such as lymphoma of the small bowel. In children, undiagnosed coeliac disease can cause lack of proper development, short stature and behavioural problems.

Who is affected by coeliac disease?

People are born with a genetic predisposition to develop coeliac disease. They inherit a particular genetic make-up (HLA type) with the genes DQ2 and DQ8 being identified as the 'coeliac genes'. Pathology laboratories are able to test for these genes, however, the test can only exclude coeliac disease, not diagnose it.
A first-degree relative (parent, brother, sister, child) of someone with coeliac disease has about a 10% chance of also having the disease. If one identical twin has coeliac disease, there is a 70% chance that the other twin will also be affected (but not necessarily diagnosed at the same time). Environmental factors also play an important role in the development of coeliac disease.

Coeliac disease can also be associated with other autoimmune conditions such as:

- type 1 diabetes
- autoimmune thyroid disease
- pernicious anaemia
- rheumatoid arthritis
- inflammatory bowel disease, and
- lupus.

A causative link has not been proven, but having one genetic autoimmune disease increases the risk of having another.

Symptoms of coeliac disease

The underlying genetic predisposition to develop coeliac disease is present at birth. Coeliac disease was once considered to be a childhood condition, which only produced symptoms in very young children. Nowadays, people accept that coeliac disease may be triggered at any time from infancy to senior years. Some infants become rapidly and severely ill when foods containing gluten are introduced into their diet; other children develop problems slowly over several years. Many have few or no problems during childhood but only develop symptoms as adults.

The symptoms of coeliac disease can range from severe to minor or atypical and can even be clinically silent. Some symptoms might be confused with irritable bowel syndrome or a food intolerance, while others may be put down to stress, or getting older. As a consequence, it may take some time before an accurate diagnosis is even sought, let alone made.

The following symptoms of coeliac disease might occur singularly or in combination:

- Fatigue, weakness and lethargy
- Anaemia
- Flatulence
- Abdominal swelling or bloating
- Diarrhoea—can be quite severe but may not necessarily be obvious
- Constipation—sometimes experienced instead of diarrhoea, although many people do not experience either while some experience both
- Cramping and bloating
- Nausea and vomiting
- Weight loss—although many people do not lose weight and some even gain weight

Less common symptoms in adults

- Easy bruising of the skin
- Recurrent mouth ulcers and/or swelling of mouth or tongue
- Infertility or miscarriages
- Low calcium levels
- Vitamin deficiencies
- Skin rashes—such as dermatitis herpetiformis
- Dental defects
- Altered mental alertness
- Bone and joint pains

Common symptoms in children

- Abdominal distention, pain and flatulence

- Nausea and vomiting

- Diarrhoea or constipation

- Large, bulky, foul stools (steatorrhea)

- Poor weight gain

- Weight loss in older children

- Delayed growth or delayed puberty

- Tiredness

- Anaemia

- Irritability

Many people with coeliac disease are 'asymptomatic', that is they have no gastrointestinal symptoms at all.

Can coeliac disease be cured?

People with coeliac disease remain sensitive to gluten throughout their life, so in a sense they are never cured. However, once gluten is removed from the diet, the small bowel lining steadily repairs itself and the absorption of nutrients from food returns to normal.

People with coeliac disease can enjoy a normal, healthy lifestyle provided they maintain a gluten-free diet. Relapse occurs if gluten is reintroduced.

For more information about coeliac disease, visit The Coeliac Society's website: www.coeliacsociety.com.au

Farinaceous Foods

Farinaceous foods are starchy foods that contain flour or meal. They are essential to a balanced diet. So important, in fact, that the eating patterns of most regions around the world depend on at least one type of farinaceous food for their daily carbohydrate intake and as an affordable food to satisfy the appetite.

Common farinaceous foods suitable for coeliacs and people with IBS are:

- Potatoes—floury, waxy and all-purpose

- Pulses—peas, beans and lentils

- Rice—long grain, short grain, brown or wild

- Grains—corn, buckwheat and quinoa

- Pasta—originally made from flour, is now made from a combination of gluten-free flour and gums to hold it together.

- Polenta—derived from corn and can also be ground into cornmeal; polenta can sometimes replace flour in cakes and bread.

A note on some useful ingredients

Smoking mix for Smoked Duck with Coconut Salad, see page 28.

Gums

Without wheat flour, you need to find a suitable alternative for baking, binding water and making sauces. Guar gum and xanthan gum can be used as a binding agent and in most cases, for binding water. We also use corn starch in a lot of our cooking now to help bind and thicken, but gum is about eight times stronger than corn starch and about 16 times stronger than flour.

Stock

The secret to a tasty dish is a great stock—either chicken or beef or even duck. I always make sure I make chicken stock about once a month and freeze it in 500ml clear containers. This gives me a better product and it's really cheap and easy to make. Many recipes use stock and if you can make it yourself you are always better off.

Metric units are used throughout this book.

The approximate equivalents are as follows.

solid measures

Metric	Imperial
10g	$^1/_3$oz
15g	$^1/_2$oz
20g	$^2/_3$oz
30g	1oz
45g	$1^1/_2$oz
60g	2oz
90g	3oz
100g	$3^1/_2$oz
125g	4oz
150g	5oz
165g	$5^1/_2$oz
180g	6oz
200g	$6^1/_2$oz
220g	7oz
250g	8oz
300g	10oz
350g	$11^1/_2$oz
400g	13oz
500g	1lb (16oz)
750g	$1^1/_2$ lb (24oz)
1kilogram	2lb (32oz)

liquid measures

Metric	Imperial Standard cups
5ml	1 teaspoon (tsp)
10ml	1 dessertspoon
20ml	1 fl oz
15ml	$^2/_3$fl oz
50ml	$1^3/_4$fl oz
60ml	2fl oz
80ml	$2^3/_4$fl oz
100ml	$3^1/_2$fl oz
125ml	4fl oz
185ml	6fl oz
200ml	$6^1/_2$fl oz
250ml	8fl oz
500ml	16fl oz
750ml	24fl oz
1Litre	32fl oz

oven temperatures

100°C very slow	200°F Gas Mark 1
120°C very slow	250°F Gas Mark 1
140°C slow	275°F Gas Mark 2
150°C slow	300°F Gas Mark 2
160°C warm	325°F Gas Mark 2–3
180°C moderate	350°F Gas Mark 4
190°C moderately hot	375°F Gas Mark 5
200°C hot	400°F Gas Mark 6
220°C hot	420°F Gas Mark 7
230°C very hot	450°F Gas Mark 8
240°C very hot	475°F Gas Mark 8–9
250°C very hot	485°F Gas Mark 9
260°C very hot	500°F Gas Mark 10

My Homestyle

Cooking

Starters

Crispy Prawn Noodle Salad
with tamarind dressing

INGREDIENTS

100g (3½oz) packet mung bean noodles

1 egg white

4 green prawns (shrimp), cleaned

1 Lebanese cucumber, thinly sliced

½ lemongrass, white part only, thinly sliced

½ daikon, or red radish, thinly sliced

100g (3½oz) dried coconut, thinly sliced

1 bunch coriander (cilantro)

1 bunch mint

2 kaffir lime leaves

1⅕L (40fl oz) oil for frying

DRESSING

25g (1oz) fresh ginger, peeled and coarsely chopped

2 cups palm sugar

1 small chilli

¼ teaspoon sesame seeds, crushed

1 cup tamarind pulp

1 cup soy sauce

5 limes, juiced

1 tablespoon fish sauce

SPECIAL EQUIPMENT

Electric thermometer

Cut the mung bean noodles into 2cm (¾in) strips with a sharp knife or scissors. Whisk egg white and dip prawns into the egg white, then roll them into the noodles until covered. Set aside.

Combine cucumber, lemongrass, daikon or radish, coconut, coriander, mint and lime leaves.

Heat oil in a deep fryer or a large pot to approximately 180°C (350°F). The hotter the better for cooking prawns. Add prawns, cook for about 30–40 seconds then carefully remove prawns using a slotted spoon. Drain prawns on paper towel, pat off the excess fat and sprinkle with salt.

To make the dressing, whiz all dressing ingredients, except fish sauce, in a blender or food processor until smooth. Gradually add fish sauce, adjusting to your personal taste. Remember—fish sauce can be very salty! This dressing is very fragrant, spicy and tangy; it should have enough lime to complement your dish.

Place the salad ingredients into a bowl and pour over the dressing. Remember to dress salad just before serving, otherwise the leaves will wilt from the highly acidic dressing.

Serve prawns on top of the salad, with a fresh slice of lime.

CHEF'S NOTES:

With this authentic Thai-style dressing, you can use a mortar and pestle to crush the herbs and spices together to make a paste before adding the liquids. However, if you don't have a mortar and pestle, a blender has the same effect. If you find the dressing too spicy, add more palm sugar.

Seared Scallops
with cheesy polenta and chorizo

INGREDIENTS

10 shallots (spring onion)

50g (2¼oz) butter

4⅕L (1 gallon) chicken stock

500g (1lb) buckwheat polenta

500g (1lb) parmesan cheese

Pepper, to taste

5 button mushrooms

Olive oil

2⅕L (64fl oz) white wine

2 sprigs thyme

1 bayleaf

1⅕L (38fl oz) cream

Salt

1 lemon

1 chorizo sausage

30 scallops

1 punnet shiso micro herbs (garnish only)

Dice 2 shallots and sauté with butter until soft. Add half the chicken stock and bring to the boil. Add the polenta to the boiled liquid, frequently whisking to prevent lumps from forming. Cook until smooth and creamy—this should take around 5 minutes.

Add the parmesan and pepper. Cover with cling wrap just touching the top of the polenta. This should stop it from getting a skin and also keep it warm. Set aside.

Slice the rest of the shallots and the mushrooms. Fry with a little olive oil until fragrant, then add the white wine and the rest of the chicken stock. Add the thyme and bay leaf.

Cook until liquid in mixture is reduced to approximately 100ml (3fl oz) or half a cup. Once reduced, add the cream and bring it to the boil. Strain the sauce and season with salt and juice from the lemon.

Slice the chorizo sausage into 5cm (2in) long batons, then fry in a hot frypan with the scallops until scallops are golden brown on both sides.

Serve polenta topped with scallops and chorizo. Garnish with shiso herbs.

CHEF'S NOTES:

It's important the scallops don't over cook, or they will become very dry and rubbery. Shiso herbs are a member of the mint family and were first grown in China and Japan.

Goat's Curd and Beetroot Salad
with braised lentils

INGREDIENTS

1x300g (10oz) can cooked green lentils, drained

20ml (¾fl oz) olive oil

20ml (¾fl oz) champagne vinegar

1 bunch continental parsley

1 small raw beetroot

100g (3½oz) goat's curd

Baby coriander (cilantro), to garnish

Combine lentils, olive oil and champagne vinegar in a dish. Marinate 10 minutes. Wash parsley and, sprinkle leaves over the lentil mixture.

Cut beetroot into 1cm (½in) thick slices and shape using a 5cm round cutter. In a pot of cold water, bring beetroot slices to the boil. Cook for approximately 5 minutes then drain.

Serve the beetroot in the middle of the plate, scoop lentil mixture over the beetroot and top with a generous dollop of the goat's curd.

Garnish with some baby coriander and some excess liquid from the lentils.

Smoked Duck
with coconut salad

Serves 2

INGREDIENTS
1 duck breast, skin on

SMOKING MIX
50g (2oz) brown sugar
50g (2oz) loose-leaf jasmine tea
50g (2oz) long grain rice
25g (¾oz) pickled ginger

SALAD
½ bunch mint, leaves only
50g (2oz) daikon, julienned
50g (2oz) coconut, shaved
(use fresh coconut, if available)
1 stick lemongrass, shredded finely
2 kaffir lime leaves, julienned
1 lebanese cucumber, shaved
20g (2/3oz) unsalted cashews

DRESSING
1 garlic clove, crushed
½ small chilli, crushed
2 limes, juiced
30ml (1fl oz) fish sauce
¼ block (about 30g or 1oz)
palm sugar, grated
30ml (1fl oz) sugar syrup

SPECIAL EQUIPMENT
Aluminium Foil

Score the duck's skin, very lightly, to help with the rendering process. This releases the fat from the skin and helps it go crispy.

To make the smoking mix, combine all smoking mix ingredients in a bowl, add a little water and mix until it resembles wet sand. This will stop the smoking mix from catching alight. Make a foil parcel by folding about 50cm (20ins) of foil over itself about 4 times. This will thicken the foil to stop it from melting. Now place the smoking mixture on one side of the foil, folding the other half over the mix and press the edges all around so the smoke mix is enclosed. Score the top of the foil parcel to let out the smoke.

Place the foil parcel in a frypan and heat until smoke comes out of the foil (this should take about 5 minutes). Once the parcel starts smoking, lay the duck on a wire rack above the smoking mix parcel, skin side up. Cover with a lid and turn the heat off. Duck must be smoked for only 8 minutes, otherwise it will become bitter. The duck won't be fully cooked at this smoking stage.

Once the duck has been smoked, it can then be cooked in a frying pan, skin side down, until crispy. This should take a further 5 minutes, which will cook the duck so that it's just pink. Set duck aside to rest for 5 minutes.

Meanwhile, combine mint, daikon, coconut, lemongrass, lime leaves, cucumber and cashews.

To prepare dressing, whiz all dressing ingredients in a food processor or blender until smooth. Pour over the finished salad and toss lightly. Serve duck, sliced, with coconut salad.

Artichoke and Olive Tart

INGREDIENTS

100g (3½oz) savoury pastry (see short crust pasty recipe, page 107 baking)

1⅓kg (2lb10oz) raw Jerusalem artichokes

600ml (20fl oz) water

600ml (20fl oz) milk

1 lemon

6 eggs

4 egg yolks, extra

900 ml (30fl oz) cream

30 olives, pitted and chopped

100gm (3½oz) rocket

20ml (1fl oz) extra virgin olive oil

20ml (1fl oz) lemon juice

Preheat oven to 140°C (230°F/Gas Mark 2).

Roll pastry out to around 5mm (1/10in) thick. Press into a springform tin or a flan tin with a loose bottom. (I use a 10cm or 4ins flan tin for this recipe.)

Prick pastry a few times with a fork. This allows the steam to escape when cooking. Cook in oven for 25 minutes until crisp.

For the filling, peel the artichokes and, in a large pot, combine with water, milk and a squeeze of lemon. This will help stop any further discolouration. Simmer for 20 minutes or until soft.

Drain artichokes and puree in a blender or food processor until smooth. Whisk eggs and egg yolks in a bowl until smooth. While the artichokes are still warm, add the eggs to the puree and set aside to cool.

Whip the cream until it starts to thicken and look like waves. Fold cream and olives into the cooled puree and season with salt and pepper. Cook in oven for 30 minutes or until the egg mixture sets. Refrigerate until ready to serve.

Serve wedges of the tart next to rocket drizzled with olive oil and lemon juice.

CHEF'S NOTES:
The baked pastry can be stored in an airtight container or frozen for 3–4 weeks.

Egg and Bacon Omelette

INGREDIENTS

1 red onion, diced

2 rashers bacon, rind removed

½ clove garlic, sliced thinly

2 tomatoes, diced

4 eggs, lightly beaten

50g (2oz) mozzarella

50g (2oz) rocket

30ml (1fl oz) balsamic vinegar

60ml (2fl oz) olive oil

Preheat oven to 180ºC (350ºF/Gas Mark 4).

In a non-stick frypan, sauté the onion, garlic and bacon until it becomes fragrant and lightly coloured. Combine eggs and chopped tomato into a bowl and pour it into the pan. Transfer to a baking dish and sprinkle with mozzarella. Cook in the oven with a sprinkle of the mozzarella cheese for 5–6 minutes. Do not overcook as eggs will become rubbery.

Serve omelette topped with rocket and drizzled with vinegar and olive oil.

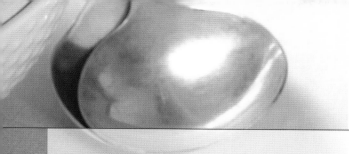

INGREDIENTS

1x400g (13oz) packet split peas

1¾kg (3¾lb) ham hocks, strings removed

VEGETABLE MIREXPOIX

1 carrot, peeled and chopped

2 stalks celery, chopped

1 leek, white part only, thinly sliced

1 brown onion, chopped

1 bay leaf

1 sprig fresh thyme

2L (64fl oz) chicken stock

salt and pepper

HAM HOCK CANNELLONI

3 chicken breasts, skin removed and coarsely chopped

300ml (10fl oz) cream

½ bunch parsley, chopped

Pinch cayenne pepper

Reserved ham hock meat (from soup)

100g (3½oz) dried lasagne sheets

1 teaspoon sour cream (optional)

For the soup, combine peas, ham and vegetables for mirexpoix in a large pot. Bring to the boil, reduce heat and simmer about 4 hours.

Using a slotted spoon, remove the hocks from the soup. Separate meat from the hock and discard bones. Chop meat coarsely and set aside for the cannelloni.

Strain soup through a sieve and season to taste.

For the cannelloni, puree the chicken breast with a pinch of salt in a food processor or blender until smooth. Add the cream, parsley and cayenne. Puree for about 30 seconds. Any more than 30 seconds will risk the mixture curdling.

Fold in the reserved ham hock meat and refrigerate.

Using a pasta machine or rolling pin, roll pasta dough to about 2mm (⅛in) thickness and cut into 10x5cm (4x2in) rectangles. Use a piping bag to pipe the mixture down the 5cm (2in) side of the pasta sheet. The mixture needs to be piped about 2cm (¾in) thick. Roll the pasta sheet over to enclose filling. Pinch the ends of the pasta to stop the mixture from escaping.

Cook cannelloni in boiling water for 2–3minutes. Meanwhile, re-heat soup and pour into a large bowl. Add cannelloni and garnish with extra parsley and sour cream, if desired.

CHEF'S NOTES:

Mirexpoix is a French word for chopped, mixed vegetables. When pureeing the chicken, the salt works as an abrasive which means that it will stop the chicken from becoming liquid-like. This method will also work with other meats and fish.

Coriander Crisps
with tzatziki

PASTRY

80ml (2¾fl oz) water

80g (2½oz) gluten-free cornflour

1 cup fresh coriander leaves

20g (1oz) sesame seeds

100g (4oz) rice flour

1 teaspoon baking powder

1 teaspoon salt

TZATZIKI

1 Lebanese cucumber

100g (3½oz) Greek yoghurt

1 clove garlic, chopped finely

½ bunch mint leaves

40ml (1¼fl oz) lemon juice

Preheat oven to 200°C (400°F/Gas mark 6).

Combine the water and cornflour in a saucepan and bring to the boil, stirring constantly. This will turn into a paste quickly. Once it has, remove from heat and combine mixture with coriander, sesame seeds, rice flour, baking powder and salt until smooth. The dough shouldn't be sticky, but it shouldn't be completely dry either.

Using a pasta machine or rolling pin, roll the dough out paper-thin and cut into desired shapes. Brush with olive oil and cook in oven, on non-stick paper, about 15 minutes. Set aside to cool.

For the tzatziki, grate the cucumber into a clean cloth and add pinch of salt to it. Now squeeze the cucumber, still in the cloth, to remove the excess liquid. In a bowl, combine cucumber, yoghurt, garlic and mint. Add lemon juice to taste until desired tartness is achieved.

CHEF'S NOTES:
You can make the pastry, then wrap it in cling wrap and store it in the freezer for future use. Removing the excess liquid from the cucumber will stop tzatziki from becoming too runny.

Crab and Asparagus Omelette
with watercress salad

INGREDIENTS

6 spears fresh asparagus, peeled if necessary

3 eggs, lightly beaten

¼ bunch chives, chopped finely

1 teaspoon tarragon, chopped finely

50ml (2oz) cream

Salt and pepper, to taste

½ teaspoon olive oil

50g (2oz) cooked crab meat

WATERCRESS SALAD

1 bunch watercress, leaves only

2 shallots, peeled and shaved

2 tomatoes, diced

20ml (1fl oz) olive oil

20ml (1fl oz) lemon juice

Cook asparagus in boiling water for about 30 seconds. Refresh in ice-cold water to retain the green colour and stop it from over-cooking.

Combine eggs with herbs and cream. Season with pepper. Heat the oil in a non-stick pan and add egg mixture, swirling to help the egg cook quickly.

When the omelette is half-cooked, add asparagus and crab meat in the middle and fold ends over to achieve a cigar shape.

For the salad, wash the watercress and drain. Combine in a bowl with the rest of the salad ingredients and serve with the omelette.

CHEF'S NOTES:
Avoid adding salt to the eggs early on as it has a burning affect and will turn them brown if added too soon.

Mains

Prawn and Saffron Risotto

INGREDIENTS

Pinch saffron threads

1L (32fl oz) white wine

2L (64fl oz) chicken stock

1 tablespoon olive oil

1 clove garlic, crushed

10 shallots, diced finely

1kg (2lb) aborio rice

20 large prawns, shelled and de-veined

1 bay leaf

2 sprigs thyme

½ bunch chopped chives

1 lemon rind, grated

Soak saffron in the wine for 3 minutes.

In a large saucepan, bring chicken stock to the boil, remove from heat and set aside.

Heat oil in a frypan and cook garlic and shallots until fragrant. Add rice, stir and cook for 2 minutes or until rice starts to become translucent.

Add white wine and cook approximately 10 minutes or until the wine is evaporated. Gradually add a little hot chicken stock at a time, stirring between additions, until rice is cooked through. Add bay leaf and thyme.

When rice is cooked, add the prawns, chives and lemon rind. Add water to adjust the consistency until it is soft and fluffy.

CHEF'S NOTES:

Instead of stirring continuously, you can shake the pan to mix the rice. This will avoid 'sticky' rice.

Tea-smoked Atlantic Salmon
with wombok salad

INGREDIENTS

2 x 200g (6½oz) fillets Atlantic salmon

SMOKING MIX

200g (6½oz) jasmine rice

4 tea bags (green tea flavour)

50g (2oz) soft brown sugar

1 cinnamon stick

SALAD

1 wombok (Chinese cabbage), shredded

1 red onion, finely chopped

4 Roma tomatoes, coarsely chopped

1 bunch coriander (cilatro), roughly torn

1 carrot, grated

60ml (2fl oz) olive oil

60ml (2fl oz) lemon juice

Salt and pepper

SPECIAL EQUIPMENT

Deep roasting tray with lid for smoking

1 wire rack that fits into deep roasting tray

Aluminium foil

Rub salmon with some oil and then season with salt and pepper.

To make the smoking mix, mix rice, tea bags, brown sugar and a cinnamon stick together in a bowl with a little water to moisten. Adding the water will stop it from burning too much while getting the flavour correct.

Place the smoking mix in a large piece of foil that you can fold into a little parcel. Slice a few slits on the top of the smoking foil parcel.

Put your smoking mix parcel into a deep roasting tray on high heat, to create its own natural smoking effect. Once it begins smoking, place the salmon fillets on a wire rack above the smoking mix parcel.

Cover the tray to trap the smoke. Immediately reduce the heat by half, so that the fish doesn't dry out. Once the heat is reduced, leave the fish to cook for 3 minutes, then remove from heat and leave, covered, for 10 minutes. This will be enough to cook the fish so that it's just pink inside. If you would like your fish more orange and cooked through, cook for 10 minutes, then remove from heat and rest it for 10 minutes.

To make the salad, chop and combine wombok, onion, tomato, coriander and carrot. Make a dressing by combining the olive oil and lemon juice.

Serve salad topped with warm salmon.

Almond Chicken Curry

INGREDIENTS

1 tablespoon ghee (clarified butter)

2 teaspoons ground cumin seeds

4 cloves, ground

12 fresh curry leaves

4 green cardamom pods, bruised

2 cloves garlic, crushed

2 long red chillis

1 teaspoon ground turmeric

1 brown onion, finely chopped

12 chicken thigh fillets, chopped into cubes

½ cup (4fl oz) coconut cream

2x400g (13oz) cans crushed tomatoes

1 teaspoon garam masala

100g (3½oz) almond meal

1 cup (8fl oz) fresh coconut

50g (2¼oz) flaked almonds, to garnish

In a large saucepan over medium heat, melt ghee. Add cumin seeds, cloves, curry leaves, cardamom, garlic, chilli, turmeric and onion. Cook for 5 minutes or until onion softens.

Add the chicken and reduce the heat. Cook, stirring occasionally, for 30 minutes. Add the cream and canned tomatoes. Cook for 15–20 minutes or until the sauce thickens slightly. Remove from heat. Stir in the garam masala, almond meal and fresh coconut.

Sprinkle curry with flaked almonds and serve with rice and raita (if desired).

CHEF'S NOTES:
Raita is a refreshing Indian accompaniment to spicy curries and is made from chopped cucumber mixed with plain yoghurt.

Pork Loin
with quinoa and apples

INGREDIENTS

130g (4½oz) quinoa

160ml (5¼fl oz) boiling water

2 tablespoons prunes, pitted and finely chopped

2 teaspoons pine nuts, toasted

2 tablespoons fresh coriander (cilantro), coarsely chopped

2 tablespoons fresh flat-leaf parsley, coarsely chopped

500g (1lb), boneless pork loin, rind on

2½ cups (20fl oz) apple cider

2 medium apples, peeled, cored and sliced thickly

1 large red onion, cut into thick wedges

2 tablespoons brown sugar

Preheat oven to 180°C (350°F/Gas Mark 4).

In a heatproof bowl, combine quinoa and boiling water. Cover and stand for about 5 minutes or until the water is absorbed, fluffing occasionally with a fork. Stir in prunes, nuts, coriander and parsley.

Place pork on a chopping board and remove any excess fat. Slice through thickest part of the meat horizontally, without cutting through to the other side. Open pork out (like a book) to form one large piece and press 1 cup of the quinoa mixture down one side of the loin. Roll pork to enclose stuffing, securing with kitchen string at 2cm (¾in) intervals.

Place pork on an oven rack, in a large shallow flameproof baking dish. Pour 2 cups of cider over the pork. Roast, uncovered, about 50 minutes or until cooked through. Remove pork from baking dish and cover to keep warm. Reserve liquid in the dish.

Cook remaining quinoa mixture in small ovenproof dish, covered, about 10 minutes or until heated through. Meanwhile, transfer the liquid from the baking dish into a pan. Add remaining cider, apple, onion and sugar. Cook on medium heat, stirring until apple is just tender. Serve sliced pork with apple mixture and quinoa.

CHEF'S NOTES:
We used Granny Smith apples in this recipe. You can ask your butcher to remove any excess fat and to butterfly the pork for you.

Truffle Risotto
with braised rabbit

INGREDIENTS

RABBIT BRAISE

1 whole rabbit (preferably locally farmed)

40ml (1¼fl oz) olive oil

1 carrot, roughly chopped

2 sticks celery, roughly chopped

150ml (5fl oz) white wine

2L (64fl oz) chicken stock, hot

6 tomatoes

RISOTTO

1 clove garlic

40ml (1¼fl oz) olive oil

2 shallots (spring onions), diced finely

½ onion, diced finely

80g (2½oz) arborio rice

50ml (1¾fl oz) dry white wine

1 bay leaf

5g (¼oz) whole black winter truffles

Rabbit Braise

Ask your butcher to cut the rabbit into 3 parts, keeping the rear legs, front legs and mid area separate as they will all be cooked at different times.

Preheat oven to 140°C (280°F/gas mark 2). Heat a small amount of olive oil in a frypan. It's best to use a frying or braising dish which you can also bake in, such as deep pot with heat proof handles or a casserole dish.

Fry the rabbit with the carrot and celery until rabbit is golden brown. Add the white wine and hot chicken stock so that the liquid half-covers the rabbit. Bring mixture to the boil.

Cook in oven, covered, around 40 minutes.

The mid area (rib) of the rabbit should take approximately 30 minutes to cook. When the rib/middle area of the rabbit has started to come away from the bone, take this section out of the liquid and set aside.

As the rib area of the rabbit begins to cool, remove the meat carefully in large pieces and pour over a little braising liquid. This will keep the rabbit from drying out.

Once the legs are also tender and coming away from the bone, remove the meat in large pieces and add to the braising liquid with the rib meat.

Strain the excess liquid from the braised rabbit; refrigerate the meat and set aside the liquid—it can be used to help cook the risotto base.

Risotto

Peel the garlic but don't chop it—leave it whole so you can remove it later.

Heat olive oil in a large frypan with a little salt. Sauté the shallots, onion and garlic for 3–4 minutes until translucent. Add rice. This is a very critical moment as the rice must be dry fried without scorching. The key to getting this right is allowing the rice to be become clear, which will happen quickly, so be ready!

Once the rice is clear, add the wine. This process is known as deglazing and transfers the beautiful flavours from the pan into the rice.

At this stage you should have a rice and shallot mixture with an intense white wine smell reducing in your pan. Once the wine has almost reduced away, add the bay leaf.

Reduce the heat and gradually add the reserved braising liquid. Adding this stock little by little will allow you to control the amount of liquid that is cooking into your rice.

As the rice becomes larger and fluffy, check it closely. Stir the rice constantly and don't let it stick to the bottom. To check if your rice is cooked, place one small grain on the bench and squash it, using a spoon.

Once the rice is cooked, slice the truffles using a sharp knife or a truffle slicer. Add them to the cooked rice and reserve some for a garnish. Place the rabbit into the hot rice to warm up and add a little more stock or water.

The risotto should be quite creamy and soft; if it's too dry, add some more liquid to suit.

Serve risotto garnished with truffles.

CHEF'S NOTES:

Braise means to slow cook in the oven half covered with liquid. The risotto base recipe, minus the truffles, can be used for any other risotto.

Italian Sausage Ragout
with penne

INGREDIENTS

10 spicy Italian sausages

1kg (2lb) canned crushed tomatoes

1L (32fl oz) water

Extra water, if needed

500g (1lb) gluten-free penne

200g (6½oz) parmesan, shaved

Split the skins of the sausages and remove the meat. Combine meat with tomatoes and water in a large pot. Using your hands, squeeze the mixture together. This will give a smooth texture and allow all the spices to blend into the tomato.

Bring it to the boil, then reduce heat and simmer, until slow bubbles form and liquid reduces. If your sausage is still a little rubbery, cook it for a little longer, topping up the water if necessary. This should take about 1½–2 hours. Once the sausages have a shiny appearance, remove the pot from the heat.

Meanwhile, cook pasta separately following packet directions. Drain, and stir into sauce just before serving.

Serve pasta topped with parmesan.

CHEF'S NOTES:

This is probably the easiest Italian sausage ragout you'll ever make. If my kids can make this, you can! The sausage meat is a combination of pork and beef with some spices and salt. There are two types available — hot or mild — I use the hot variety. I have had this sauce tasted by some very reputable Italian chefs and they have said it is better than their nonna's cooking, but shhh… it's a secret!

Seafood Paella

INGREDIENTS

1L (32fl oz) fish stock

1 teaspoon saffron threads (or powder)

2 tablespoons olive oil

250g (8oz) firm white fish fillets, cut into 2cm (¾in) pieces

1 brown onion, finely chopped

2 cloves garlic, crushed

2 cups long grain rice

2 tomatoes, peeled, deseeded, diced

2 teaspoons smoked paprika

500g (1lb) medium green king prawns, peeled and de-veined

150g (5oz) baby squid, cleaned, cut into 1cm (½in) thick rings

12 mussels, scrubbed and de-bearded

²/₃ cup frozen peas

In a saucepan over medium heat, combine fish stock, a little water and saffron. Bring to the boil then remove from heat. Cover to keep warm.

Meanwhile, heat 1 tablespoon of oil in a large non-stick frypan over medium-high heat. Add fish and cook for 1 minute each side or until lightly golden. Transfer to a plate and cover to keep warm.

Add remaining oil to pan with onion and garlic. Cook for 5 minutes or until soft. Add rice, tomatoes and smoked paprika. Stir to combine. Using a wooden spoon, spread mixture evenly over base of pan.

Add half of the stock mixture to frying pan and bring back to the boil. Shake pan to spread mixture across pan (do not stir). Reduce heat to medium and cook, uncovered, without stirring, for 10 minutes or until stock is absorbed.

Add prawns, squid and mussels, pressing into rice mixture. Add ½ a cup stock mixture and cook until all the liquid is absorbed. Repeat with remaining stock mixture, ½ a cup at a time, adding fish and peas with the last ½ cup of stock. This process should take about 15–20 minutes. Remove from the heat and stand, covered, for 5 minutes. Serve seasoned with pepper.

CHEF'S NOTES:

Traditionally, this recipe is made using Bomba rice, a special type of Spanish rice that is long grain, but also fat, so it can cook for hours and absorb all the liquid and flavours of the paella without burning! It is known as the 'King' of rice.

Prosciutto-wrapped Lamb
with gremolata mash

INGREDIENTS

300g (10oz) rock salt, for roasting potatoes

500g (1lb) pontiac potatoes

100g (3½oz) butter

200ml (6½fl oz) cream

1 bunch fresh flat-leaf parsley, finely chopped

2 lemons, juice and zest

Salt and pepper

¼ cup olive oil

100g (3½oz) chicken wings

10 shallots (spring onion), peeled and thinly sliced

2 carrots, peeled and coarsely chopped

200ml (6½fl oz) madeira wine

1L (32fl oz) chicken stock

1L (32fl oz) veal stock

2 whole lamb racks

4 slices pancetta

CHEF'S NOTES:
The leftover potato skins make a great snack—instead of throwing them away, heat them up in the oven with a little cayenne pepper and salt and serve them with sour cream. Yum!

Preheat oven to 200ºC (400ºF/Gas Mark 6).

In a roasting tray, combine rock salt and potatoes. Cook in oven, about 30 minutes or until they are very soft in the middle and crunchy on top. While the potatoes are still hot, cut in half and scoop out the middle flesh. Squash the potatoes through a drum sieve or, alternatively, use a masher. Discard skins.

Heat the butter and cream in a pot and bring to the boil. Add this to the mashed potato, mixing quickly to avoid lumps. This must be done as soon as possible, if the potatoes become cold, they will start to go gluey. Once the mashed potato is creamy, add the chopped parsley, lemon juice, lemon zest, salt and pepper. Cover to keep warm.

Heat olive oil in a large pan. Add chicken wings, shallots and carrots. Cook until all the ingredients are golden brown, add the madeira and cook until reduced to a sticky glaze. Add the chicken and veal stock and cook until liquid is reduced by approximately 70%.

Strain mixture and reserve liquid. Remove 3 of the 4 bones of each lamb rack, leaving one bone per rack. In a hot frypan heat a few drops of olive oil, cook the lamb until coloured all over. Remove from heat, transfer to a baking dish and wrap two pieces of pancetta around the middle meat area. This will help keep it moist while roasting.

Cook lamb in oven at about 140ºC (270ºF/Gas Mark 1) for approximately 15 minutes or until cooked as desired. Once the lamb is cooked, remove from oven and cover to keep warm.

Serve lamb on top of mashed potato drizzled with sauce.

54   My Homestyle Cooking: Mains

Chicken Paillard
with spicy white polenta

Serves: 2

INGREDIENTS

200g (6½oz) chicken fillet, trimmed

½ cup Greek yoghurt

10g (⅓oz) ground cumin

10g (⅓oz) ground turmeric

Pinch chilli powder

30ml (1fl oz) olive oil

POLENTA

50ml (1⅔fl oz) olive oil

1 clove garlic, finely diced

1 red onion, finely chopped

10g (⅓oz) ground turmeric

1 stick cinnamon

1 lemon rind, grated

500ml (16fl oz) chicken stock

200g (6½oz) fine white polenta

1 bunch parsley, chopped roughly

Lemon wedges, to garnish

Preheat oven to 180°C (350°F/Gas Mark 4).

Slice chicken fillet in half horizontally around the thickest part and open out (like a book) to one large, flat piece.

Combine yoghurt, cumin, turmeric, chilli powder and oil in a large ceramic dish. Season with a little salt and pepper. Coat chicken in yoghurt mixture and refrigerate for 10 minutes.

In a non-stick frypan, cook the chicken until sealed (or lightly browned). Transfer to a baking dish and cook in oven for about 7 minutes.

Meanwhile, to make polenta, heat the oil in a deep saucepan over medium heat. Add onion and garlic and cook for 3 minutes, stirring occasionally until tender. Add turmeric, cinnamon and a little grated lemon rind. Stir until combined. Add chicken stock and bring to the boil. Quickly stir in the polenta, otherwise lumps will form. Cook for 6–7 minutes.

Remove the polenta from the heat and cover to keep warm. Stand 5 minutes, then stir with a spoon to keep it creamy. Do not let the polenta cool down or it will harden. Discard the cinnamon stick just before serving.

Serve polenta topped with chicken fillets and garnished with parsley and lemon wedges.

CHEF'S NOTES:
If you are using a coarser style of polenta, it will take about 10 minutes to cook.

Whole Baked Snapper
in banana leaves

INGREDIENTS

3kg (6lb) whole snapper, gutted and scaled

20g (1oz) galangal or ginger (about 2cm or ¾in), grated

2 sticks of lemongrass, sliced

2 heads whole garlic, halved

1 bunch coriander (cilantro) roots

2 whole lemons, juice and zest

MARINADE

2 cloves of garlic

25g (1oz) ginger

5 medium green chillies

100ml (3fl oz) oyster sauce,

50ml (1¾fl oz) soy sauce

100g (4oz) light palm sugar

1 lime, juiced

10 kaffir lime leaves, shredded

20g (1oz) white pepper

SPECIAL EQUIPMENT

Banana leaves, vine leaves or baking paper

Preheat oven to 180°C (350°F/Gas mark 4).

Firstly, make the marinade by crushing garlic, ginger and chillies into a paste using a mortar and pestle or bar blender, adding a little salt to help break down the hard ingredients. Add other marinade ingredients and grind to a paste.

Fill fish cavity with galangal or ginger, lemongrass, garlic, coriander and lemon. Score the side of the fish with 4 parallel cuts. After making the marinade, rub it into the sliced fish, covering the whole outside surface.

Wrap the fish in the banana leaves, anchoring with skewers and cook in oven for about half an hour.

Open the banana leaves and check that flesh of the fish is firm, which is an indication that it is ready to eat. Remember to be careful of the bones while eating, as there are many.

Chicken in a Bag

INGREDIENTS

2 baby potatoes

20ml (¾fl oz) olive oil

30g (1oz) salt

200g (6½oz) chicken breast, skin removed

1 clove garlic, chopped finely

4 basil leaves

1 chorizo sausage, sliced thickly

1 tomato, sliced thickly

50g (2oz) cumin seeds

100g (3½oz) natural yoghurt

20ml (¾fl oz) lemon juice

½ bunch fresh, flat-leaf parsley, chopped coarsely

SPECIAL EQUIPMENT

1 sheet silicone paper

Aluminium foil

Preheat oven to 180ºC (330ºF/Gas Mark 4).

Place a large square of silicone paper over a square of aluminium foil.

Slice potatoes and place them on one side of the paper. Drizzle with half the olive oil and half the salt.

Place the chicken breast on top of potatoes. Using a mortar and pestle, crush garlic and basil to create a paste. Spread paste on chicken—this will create a beautiful crust.

Top chicken with chorizo and tomato.

Drizzle with the rest of the olive oil and salt.

Fold the other half of the paper over and crimp the edges to close the bag. This will create steam when roasting in the oven to keep it moist. Cook bag in oven for approximately 25 minutes. Remove from oven and leave to stand for 5 mintues before opening bag carefully.

Meanwhile, heat a non-stick frypan and cook cumin seeds for a few minutes or until fragrant. Blend in a spice grinder or mortar and pestle until smooth. Push seeds through a sieve and mix with yoghurt, lemon juice and salt to taste.

Serve chicken on top of yoghurt sauce, garnished with parsley.

Marinated Lamb Kebabs
with greek salad

INGREDIENTS

400g (13oz) lamb shoulder, diced into 2cm cubes

2 cloves garlic, crushed

2 tablespoons olive oil

1 tablespoon dried oregano

1 tablespoon sweet paprika

1 tablespoon lemon juice

Lebanese bread, to serve

100g (3½oz) Greek yoghurt

2 lemon wedges

GREEK SALAD

1 red capsicum (bell pepper), roasted, peeled and sliced

2 green capsicums, thinly sliced horizontally

2 Lebanese cucumbers, coarsely chopped

200g (6½oz) cherry tomatoes, quartered

1 small red onion, sliced thinly

95g (3oz) small black olives

100g (3½oz) feta, crumbled

30ml (1fl oz) extra virgin olive oil

Oregano

SPECIAL EQUIPMENT

12 metal or wooden skewers

Combine the lamb, garlic, oil, oregano, paprika and lemon juice in a large bowl. Cover with cling wrap and refrigerate for 3 hours.

Meanwhile, make the Greek salad by combining capsicum, cucumber, tomato, onion, olives and feta in a large bowl. Refrigerate until required.

Thread lamb evenly along 12 soaked bamboo or metal skewers. Coat with a little olive oil and barbecue or grill skewers on medium-high heat approximately 6–8 minutes or until cooked to your liking.

Divide lamb skewers among serving plates with bread, yoghurt and lemon wedges. Serve with Greek salad drizzled with olive oil and oregano.

CHEF'S NOTES:
Always soak wooden skewers in hot water for an hour to reduce burning.

Christmas Turkey
with a twist

INGREDIENTS

1 turkey breast fillet
100g (3½oz) gluten-free plain flour
Black pepper, to taste
1 bunch picked sage leaves
10 slices prosciutto or cappacollo
50g (2oz) butter, cubed
100ml (3½fl oz) madeira wine
500ml (16fl oz) chicken stock
40g (1oz) dark chocolate (70% cocoa)
40ml (1¾fl oz) raspberry vinegar

SPATZLE (GERMAN-STYLE PASTA)

500g (1lb) gluten-free plain flour
½ teaspoon xanthan gum
½ teaspoon nutmeg
4 eggs, lightly beaten
400ml (14fl oz) full cream milk
Salt and pepper, to taste
200g (6½oz) cranberries

BRAISED RED CABBAGE

5 onions, finely sliced
100gm (3½oz) unsalted butter
1 red cabbage, sliced
6 red apples, cored and chopped coarsely
500g (1lb) currants
3 teaspoons honey
500g (1lb) brown sugar
500ml (16fl oz) chicken stock
Salt and pepper, to taste

Preheat oven to 160°C (325°F/Gas Mark 2–3).

Slice the turkey fillet in half, lengthways. Wrap in cling film and flatten slightly using a meat mallet.

Unwrap turkey, dust one side of the flattened turkey with flour and pepper.

Place 2 sage leaves and 1 slice of prosciutto on each turkey fillet.

Roll turkey to enclose filling, wrap with another slice of prosciutto and secure with a toothpick or twine.

Heat a little olive oil in a frypan and cook the rolled turkey until sealed or lightly browned. Transfer to a baking dish and cook in oven for 8 minutes.

If you have a meat thermometer, the internal temperature must reach 75°C or 135°F.

Remove the turkey from the pan and cover to keep warm. Place the pan back on the heat and add madeira wine, stirring occasionally. Once the Madeira has evaporated, add chicken stock and cook until mixture reduces by about half. Remove sauce from heat.

Set aside vinegar and chocolate until ready to serve.

Spatzle

Sift flour, gum and nutmeg in a large bowl. Add eggs and milk and whisk to combine. Season to taste with salt and pepper. Once batter is smooth, add cranberries.

Boil a large pot of water with a pinch of salt, and, using a piping bag, slowly drop portions of the mixture into it. This creates unusual strips of pasta-like shapes in the water called spatzle.

The Spatzle will rise to the top of the boiling water when cooked. Remove with a slotted spoon and refresh in ice-cold water.

Braised red cabbage

Combine sliced onions, currants and butter in a large pot. Cook, covered, on low heat until onions are translucent. Add cabbage and cook, covered a further 5 minutes, stirring occasionally. Once cabbage begins to soften, add apple and honey. Simmer until water has evaporated.

To serve, fry the spatzle in a frypan with some butter until the spatzle turns a nutty brown colour. Reheat the madeira sauce in the pan and whisk in vinegar and chocolate until chocolate has melted. Serve hot cabbage topped with sliced turkey next to spatzle drizzled with sauce.

CHEF'S NOTES:
Once cooked, the spatzle can be stored, refrigerated, for up to 4 days.

Desserts

Desserts

Apple and Rhubarb Tarte Tatin

INGREDIENTS

2 sheets gluten-free puff pastry

1 bunch rhubarb, peeled if necessary and cut into 5cm (2ins) sticks

Sugar, to sprinkle

1 vanilla bean, split in half

200g (6½oz) unsalted butter or nuttelex

200g (6½oz) caster sugar

10 red apples, peeled and cored

20g (⅔oz) icing sugar

Preheat oven to 200°C (400°F/Gas Mark 6).

Roll pastry out to approximately 5mm (⅛in) thick. Refrigerate until required.

Poach rhubarb in some water mixed with a little sugar and the vanilla bean until slightly softened.

Spread some butter evenly over the base of a heavy saucepan. Sprinkle with sugar. Add apples and rhubarb, pressing the fruit down tightly. Cook until the underside of the fruit caramelises to a deep brown.

Meanwhile, cut pastry to a slightly larger size than the pan. Cover the pastry over fruit, pressing the edges down along the inside. Cook in oven for 20–25 minutes.

Remove from heat and shake the pan gently to ensure the fruit is not stuck. Place a tray over the pan and carefully flip, so the pastry is now the base.

Place poached rhubarb on the plate with the apple tarte tatin next to it. Dust with icing sugar and serve with cream or ice cream if desired.

INGREDIENTS

2 large pineapples, peeled and sliced into 5cm (2ins) pieces

2L (64fl oz) pineapple juice

Bourbon, to taste (optional)

2 vanilla beans. split

1 large red chilli, halved lengthways

2L (64fl oz) water

PASSIONFRUIT BISCUITS

180g (6oz) unsalted butter or nuttelex

1 lemon, rind only

100g (3½oz) icing sugar

100g (3½oz) cornflour

180g (6oz) gluten-free self-raising flour

3 whole passionfruit

Preheat the oven to 150°C (300°F/Gas Mark 2).

Place slices of pineapple on a non-stick stainless steel tray. Don't use aluminium or cast iron, as there's a large amount of acid in this recipe and it might react badly to these materials.

Cover pineapple with the juice, bourbon, vanilla, chilli and water.

Cover with foil and cook in oven for 2 hours. This dish must always be covered, otherwise the sugar will burn.

Once the pineapple is tender, remove from oven, uncover dish and baste with the syrup to form a glaze. Replace the cover and set aside until ready to serve.

To make biscuits, preheat the oven to 190°C (375°F/Gas Mark 5).

Whiz all biscuit ingredients (except the passionfruit) in a food processor or blender until smooth. Pulse in the passionfruit, so you don't smash up all the pips.

Wrap in cling wrap and shape it into a cylinder. This will make it easier to make your biscuits identical. Line a flat baking tray with non-stick paper and cut biscuit mix into 2cm (¾in) thick pieces, removing cling wrap. Cook in oven for 8 minutes. Allow to cool on a wire rack.

CHEF'S NOTES:

Finding the correct pineapple is quite difficult. I look for the smallest, ripest one available, only because I like to have as little waste as possible! Do not overcook the biscuits—they will continue to cook on the wire rack.

Florentine Cheesecakes

INGREDIENTS

BASE

125g (4oz) unsalted butter or nuttelex

1 tablespoon honey

2 cups gluten-free cornflakes, roughly crushed

1¼ cups flaked almonds, toasted

¼ cup flaked or shredded coconut, toasted

1 tablespoon glace cherries, chopped

100g (3½oz) dark chocolate, melted

FILLING

60ml (2fl oz) orange juice

6 sheets gelatine leaves, softened in cold water

500g (1lb) cream cheese, at room temperature

115g (4oz) caster sugar

250ml (8fl oz) thickened cream

100g (3½oz) white chocolate, melted

2 teaspoons orange rind, finely grated

Grease and line the holes of a 12-muffin tray. Alternatively, to make one large cheesecake, use a 20cm (8ins) springform tin.

Melt butter and combine with remaining base ingredients, except the chocolate. Press mixture firmly into the base of tray or tin. Refrigerate until firm, then spread with dark chocolate. Set aside until chocolate is set.

Bring orange juice to the boil, remove from heat and set aside for 5 minutes. Dissolve the softened gelatine sheets in orange juice. Set aside to cool down, but mixture must not become completely cold, otherwise it will set.

Beat the cream cheese and sugar with an electric mixer until smooth and light. Add cream gradually until mixture is thick and smooth. On a very low speed, add the orange juice gelatine. Pour mixture into the biscuit bases and refrigerate.

Melt the white chocolate and the orange rind in a ceramic bowl in the microwave. Stir mixture with a clean spoon and drizzle over the cheesecake. Refrigerate until required and serve with berries, if desired.

'The Best' Gluten-free Chocolate Cake

INGREDIENTS

125g (4oz) soy flour (de-pitted, not compound)

110g (3¾oz) cornflour

1¼ teaspoons bicarbonate of soda

50g (2oz) pure dutch cocoa powder

275g (8½oz) caster sugar

150g (5oz) butter, melted

1 tablespoon white vinegar

1 cup (8fl oz) evaporated milk

2 eggs, lightly beaten

2 tablespoons raspberry jam

Whipped cream, to serve

Preheat oven to 180°C (350°F/Gas Mark 4).

Grease two round 22cm (8¾in) cake pans, line bases with baking paper.

Sift flours, bicarbonate of soda, cocoa powder and sugar into a large bowl. Add butter, vinegar and milk. Beat with electric mixer on low speed for 1 minute, then add eggs and jam. Beat on medium speed for 2 minutes until mixture is smooth.

Pour cake mixture into prepared tins. Cook in oven approximately 30 minutes, or until a toothpick inserted into the middle comes out almost clean. Remove from oven and stand cakes for 5 minutes before turning onto wire racks to cool.

Once cooled, sandwich the cakes together with whipped cream as the filling. Serve cake dusted with icing sugar if desired.

CHEF'S NOTES:

Make sure cornflour is 100% pure corn. As the cake mixture is rich and moist, you may find it will take longer to cook from oven to oven, so adjust cooking times to suit your oven and check with a toothpick or skewer.

Chocolate Tian
with berry sorbet and fruit coulis

INGREDIENTS

FROZEN CHOCOLATE TIAN

6 eggs

50g (2oz) icing sugar

100ml (3¼fl oz) cream

100g (4oz) dark chocolate

600ml (20fl oz) cream, extra, for whipping

BERRY SORBET

400g (13oz) sugar

100ml (3 ⅓fl oz) water

1kg (2lb) berry puree

1 vanilla bean, split

2 sticks cinnamon

FRUIT COULIS

100g (3½oz) overripe strawberries

100g (3½oz) caster sugar

CHOCOLATE TUILLE

50g (1¾oz) melted butter or nuttelex

50g (1¾oz) caster sugar

50g (1¾oz) gluten-free plain flour

50g (1¾oz) cocoa powder

2 egg whites

SPECIAL EQUIPMENT

Electronic thermometer or sugar thermometer

Whisk eggs and sugar until pale in a glass bowl set firmly on top of a saucepan of water on gentle heat. Be careful not to let the eggs go grainy, which will mean it's over cooking. If this occurs, unfortunately you will need to start again. Remove from heat and set aside to cool slightly.

Warm cream in a saucepan on medium heat. Remove from heat and stir in the chocolate, until chocolate is melted. Fold chocolate mixture into the egg mixture.

Whip the extra cream until soft peaks form, then fold through the tian mixture. Pipe mixture into cylinder moulds and freeze.

To make the sorbet, cook the sugar and water till it reaches 115°C (210°F) which is called soft boil. Remove from heat, add the puree, vanilla bean and cinnamon sticks and set aside until it cools. Once it's cooled, strain the liquid and discard the pulp. Freeze the final mixture in an ice cream churner and use machine instructions for churning times, or freeze in a tray and stir every hour until frozen.

To make the coulis, puree fruit and sugar in a food processor or blender, then strain through a sieve. Set aside until required.

To make the tuille, preheat the oven to 180°C (350°F/Gas mark 4).

Melt butter in the microwave until liquid and, if mixture is hotter than 31°C (88°F), set aside to cool to room temperature. Using an electric beater, beat sugar, flour, cocoa and egg whites until smooth. Add the cooled melted butter—if the butter is too hot it will cook the eggs and curdle the mixture.

Spread the tuille mixture about 1mm thick onto some non-stick paper. Place onto a flat baking tray and bake until golden brown. Twist the tuille into different shapes, you must do this while it is still hot from the oven—once it cools it becomes hard and crisp.

To serve, run the frozen tian under some hot water to loosen it before taking it out of the mould. Place it on one side of the plate, topped with crisp tuille. Using a hot ice cream scoop, roll a ball of the sorbet onto the frozen tian. Drizzle a few drops of the coulis on the plate and dust with icing sugar, if desired.

CHEF'S NOTES:

The coulis will keep refrigerated for 1–2 days. The unfrozen sorbet syrup is a great syrup for desserts and can kept for up to 2 weeks in the fridge.

Banana and Chocolate Soufflé

INGREDIENTS

300g (10oz) caster sugar

150ml (5fl oz) water

175g (6oz) cocoa powder

50g (2oz) gluten-free cornflour

50ml (2fl oz) brandy

2 ripe bananas

2 egg whites

30g (1oz) caster sugar

SPECIAL EQUIPMENT

Electronic thermometer

Ceramic mould, or tea cup

Preheat oven to 190°C (375°F/Gas Mark 5).

In a saucepan, boil the sugar and water until it reaches 118°C (220°F). Remove from heat.

Sift the cocoa powder and cornflour into a large bowl. Add sugar syrup, brandy and bananas. With electric beaters, mix on a medium speed until fully combined and smooth.

In a separate bowl, whisk the egg whites until they form a soft peak. Gradually add the sugar, a little at a time. Fold into cocoa mixture. Transfer to a soufflé mould or ceramic cup coated with butter and caster sugar to prevent it sticking. Cook in oven for 15–20 minutes or until souffle doubles in size. This soufflé should hold up for at least 3–5 minutes before collapsing, so serve when you are ready to eat.

Vanilla Pancakes
with strawberry sauce

INGREDIENTS

1 cup brown rice flour

1 cup white rice flour

1¼ cups rice milk

1 vanilla bean, split and scraped

2 eggs, lightly beaten

STRAWBERRY SAUCE

500g (16oz) strawberries, cleaned, hulled and coarsely chopped

300ml (10fl oz) cream

100ml (3½fl oz) skim condensed milk (about ¼ of a can)

125ml (4fl oz) lemon juice

Whiz all pancake ingredients, except eggs, in a food processor or blender until smooth. Add the eggs slowly and leave mixture to stand for 10 minutes.

Meanwhile, make the strawberry sauce. Combine strawberries, cream and condensed milk in a medium saucepan. Bring to the boil, then reduce heat and simmer 5 minutes until creamy.

Heat a little olive oil in a non-stick pan and pour about 100ml (3½fl oz) of the pancake mixture into the pan. Cook on a low-medium heat until small bubbles start to appear. Using a spatula, flip the pancake over and cook other side for a few minutes, until golden.

Serve pancakes rolled around strawberry filling with a squeeze of lemon juice.

CHEF'S NOTES:
The cooked filling can be stored in the refrigerator for up to 3 weeks.

Pizza

Basic Gluten-free Pizza Base

INGREDIENTS

200g (6½oz) white rice flour

200g (6½oz) soy flour

200g (6½oz) potato starch

125g (4oz) glutinous rice flour

50g (2oz) tapioca flour

80g (2½oz) rice bran (optional)

15g (½oz) xanthan gum

1 tablespoon sugar

15g (½oz) salt

35g (1¼oz) gluten-free baking powder

60g (2½oz) milk powder

400ml (14fl oz) water

60g (2oz) margarine

3 eggs, lightly beaten

1 teaspoon vinegar

Preheat oven to 220°C (420°F/Gas Mark 7).

In a large bowl, mix all dry ingredients. Add water, margarine, eggs and vinegar.

Mix thoroughly until smooth.

Cover and set aside until dough doubles in size. Cook in oven for approximately 10 minutes or until golden brown.

CHEF'S NOTES:
This base recipe keeps quite well and has much more taste than gluten-free white bread. I have found that using margarine instead of oil results in a slightly softer base.

Basic Tomato Sauce

INGREDIENTS

1kg (2lb) tomatoes

40ml (1 1/3 fl oz) extra virgin olive oil

1 large onion, diced

2 cloves garlic, crushed

2 tablespoons fresh basil leaves,
coarsely chopped

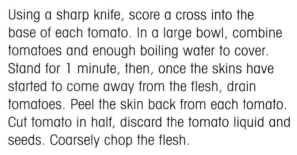

Using a sharp knife, score a cross into the base of each tomato. In a large bowl, combine tomatoes and enough boiling water to cover. Stand for 1 minute, then, once the skins have started to come away from the flesh, drain tomatoes. Peel the skin back from each tomato. Cut tomato in half, discard the tomato liquid and seeds. Coarsely chop the flesh.

In a large frypan over low heat, heat the olive oil. Add the onion and fry for 5 minutes until translucent. Add the garlic, cook for a further minute and add the tomatoes. Increase the heat, add enough water to cover the tomatoes. Bring to the boil, then reduce heat and simmer 40 minutes, stirring occasionally.

Season the sauce with salt and pepper to taste. Set aside to cool slightly, then whiz in a blender or food processor. Alternatively, press through a sauce strainer. Stir in the basil leaves.

Cool completely.

CHEF'S NOTES:
This sauce will keep refrigerated in an airtight container for up to 5 days.

Easy Ham and Mushroom Pizza

INGREDIENTS

200g (6½oz) gluten-free plain flour

100g (3½oz) vegetable margarine, cut into small cubes

300g (10oz) mashed potato (approximately 4 medium potatoes, mashed)

TOPPINGS

4 plum tomatoes, chopped coarsely

1 teaspoon tomato puree

100g gluten-free ham

1 large field mushroom

½ cup grated mozzarella cheese

Preheat oven to 200°C (400°F/Gas Mark 6). Grease a pizza plate or tin with a small amount of oil.

Sift flour into a large bowl. Rub margarine into the flour until the mixture resembles breadcrumbs. Add the mashed potato and mix thoroughly until dough forms a smooth ball.

Place half of the dough in the centre of the cooking tray or dish. Press the dough into a rough circular shape. It's a good idea to push the edges of the dough up a little—this prevents the tomatoes sliding off. Repeat with remaining dough.

Mix plum tomatoes with the tomato puree in a jug to create a sauce. Spread onto the gluten-free pizza base.

Slice ham and mushroom and lay slices on top of the tomato base. Sprinkle with cheese.

Cook in oven 10 minutes or until the pizza crust begins to turn golden.

CHEF'S NOTES:
This dough can be used to make traditional potato scones—simply add a little gluten-free baking powder to the mixture and instead of using half the dough to make a pizza base, tear off smaller bits and place 3cm (1ins) apart on a baking tray.

Mozzarella Salsiccia with Basil and Chilli

Makes 1 pizza

INGREDIENTS

100g (3½oz) basic gluten-free pizza base

100ml (3½fl oz) basic tomato sauce

1 Italian sausage, sliced

2 whole bocconcini, sliced into rounds

2 small chillies, sliced finely

½ cup fresh basil

Preheat oven to 200°C (400°F/Gas Mark 6).

Roll out the pizza base to desired thickness then place on a greased ovenproof pizza tray. Spread base evenly with tomato sauce and set aside for 5 minutes. This enables the pizza dough to 're-prove', giving the base a little more lift. Top with Italian sausage, bocconcini and chillies.

Cook in oven approximately 5 minutes or until base is crisp and sausage is browned. Serve pizza sprinkled with basil.

CHEF'S NOTES:
I like a really thin base because it's easier to roll the pizza up when eating it. It's important not to overload the toppings, they may fall off and become a little too hard to handle.

Roasted Pumpkin, Feta and Thyme

INGREDIENTS

100g (3½oz) butternut pumpkin,
diced into 5cm (2ins) cubes

1 spanish onion, quartered

100g (3½oz) basic gluten-free pizza base

50g (2oz) basic tomato sauce

50g (2oz) feta

½ bunch fresh thyme

Preheat oven to 180ºC (350ºF/Gas Mark 4).

Combine pumpkin and onion in a greased baking tray. Roast in oven approximately 15 minutes.

Roll out the pizza base to desired thickness and place dough on a greased pizza tray. Spread tomato sauce evenly around the pizza, leaving about 1cm (½in) from the edge clear. Top with pumpkin, onion and feta.

Sprinkle half the thyme over pizza and cook in oven at 200ºC (400ºF/Gas mark 6) approximately 8–10 minutes or until topping is golden brown. Serve pizza sprinkled with remaining thyme.

CHEF'S NOTES:
This pizza is very tasty and even nicer if you add a little spicy salami slices. Simply add the salami directly after the tomato sauce.

Proscuitto, Rocket and Caramelised Onion

INGREDIENTS

100g (3½oz) basic gluten-free pizza base

100g (3½oz) basic tomato sauce

50g (2oz) provelone cheese, thinly sliced

½ Spanish onion, thinly sliced

30g (1oz) fresh rocket

5 slices prosciutto

30ml (1fl oz) extra virgin olive oil.

30ml (1fl oz) balsamic vinegar

Preheat oven to 200°C (400°F/Gas mark 6).

Roll out pizza dough to desired thickness, then place onto greased pizza tray. Spread tomato sauce evenly over base, leaving a 1cm (½in) gap from the edge. Cover pizza base with provolone.

To caramelise onions, in a baking tray with a lid, combine onions with enough water to cover. Heat in oven approximately 3 minutes, uncover, then heat for another 3 minutes.

Sprinkle onions on pizza base and cook pizza in oven for 8–10 minutes.

Serve pizza topped with rocket and procuitto, drizzle with olive oil and balsamic vinegar.

Baked Apple Dessert Pizza

INGREDIENTS

100g (3½oz) basic gluten-free pizza base

100g (3½oz) crème patisserie (see chocolate eclair recipe, page 109)

2 Granny Smith apples, peeled and sliced thinly

1 lemon, juiced and rind grated

50g (2oz) brown sugar

1 cinnamon stick

50g (2oz) icing sugar for garnish

Preheat oven to 200°C (400°F/Gas mark 6).

Roll out the pizza base very thin and put it through a docking roller. Place onto a greased pizza tray. Spread the crème patisserie evenly all around the base, leaving a 1cm (½in) gap from the edge.

In a large bowl, combine apples with lemon juice, zest and sugar. Drain and spread mixture over pizza base.

Cook pizza in oven until topping is golden brown. Crumble the cinnamon over the pizza, and sprinkle with icing sugar. Serve pizza with a scoop of vanilla ice cream, if desired.

CHEF'S NOTES:
A docking roller is a roller with little pins all over, used to stop the base from rising. If you do not have a docking roller, you can use a fork to pierce holes all over the dough.

Kids' Lunches and Snacks

INGREDIENTS

1 ½ cups of mixed nuts and seeds

1 cup dried fruit (unsulfured)

¾ cup unsalted butter or nuttelex

¾ cup brown sugar or honey

Salt

1 teaspoon vanilla extract

4 cups gluten-free brown puffed rice

Line a large roasting tray with baking paper.

Pulse nuts, seeds and dried fruit in a food processor or blender until ground coarsely.

In a large saucepan, melt the butter with brown sugar or honey over low-medium heat. When the mixture is smooth and bubbling, cook for a further minute. Remove from heat, add salt and vanilla extract and stir to combine.

Use a large spatula to stir together the nuts, dried fruit and puffed rice. Stir until all ingredients are coated with the butter mixture.

Using a spatula, spread the mixture evenly into the prepared roasting tray. Cover mixture with a large piece of baking paper and use a rolling pin to smooth the top.

Cover with cling wrap and refrigerate for about 2 hours. Using a sharp knife, cut the slice in half lengthways, then cut each half into 8 pieces, about 5cm (2ins) wide.

Wrap the bars in waxed paper and store in an airtight container in the refrigerator.

CHEF'S NOTES:

Makes 16 large bars, by cutting the mixture in half lengthwise and cutting each half into 8 pieces, about 5cm wide.

Sunflower and Flaxseed Bread

INGREDIENTS

125g (4oz) white rice flour

125g (4oz) gluten-free, self-raising flour

75g (2¾oz) maize/cornflour

1 teaspoon baking powder

1 whole lemon, rind only, grated

125g (4oz) unsalted butter or nuttelex, softened

3 eggs, lightly beaten

125g (4oz) Greek yogurt

50g (2oz) sunflower seeds

20g (²/₃oz) sesame seeds

50g (2oz) flax seeds

Preheat oven to 180ºC (350ºF/Gas Mark 4).

In a large bowl, sift together flour, cornflour and baking powder. Add lemon rind and mix until completely smooth.

In a separate bowl, combine butter, eggs and yoghurt. Add this to the sifted dry ingredients and mix until smooth. This mixture doesn't need to be worked like bread. It has a different texture and will rise with the help of the eggs, instead of using yeast.

Add seeds and transfer to a greased 500g (1lb) loaf tin. Cook in oven for 35 minutes.

The bread can then be sliced and frozen to keep for breakfast or that late night snack.

CHEF'S NOTES:

Feel free to add your favourite flavours to the dough. You can add seeds, herbs or savoury purees to the mixture before baking, to create your own bread.

Almond Flour Pancakes

INGREDIENTS

1 egg, lightly beaten

90g (3oz) almond flour

50g (2oz) plain yoghurt

Butter or nuttelex for frying

¼ cup brown sugar

Combine eggs, almonds and yoghurt in a large bowl until mixture forms a batter.

Heat the butter in a small frying pan until melted. Pour in a quarter of the pancake batter. Cook on a medium heat for 1–2 minutes, or until mixture begins to set and tiny bubbles form. Using a spatula, flip pancake over to cook the other side for a further 2 minutes.

Serve pancakes sprinkled with brown sugar.

CHEF'S NOTES:

Almond flour pancakes make a great nutritious gluten-free breakfast. The quantities given will make 4 pancakes—if you are the only one eating them, you can use any remaining pancakes, cold, as a substitute for bread. Served without sugar, these pancakes are also suitable for anyone following a low carbohydrate diet.

Easy Cheesy Cornmeal Pancakes

INGREDIENTS

2 eggs, lightly beaten

¾ cup milk (or milk substitute)

½ cup rice flour

1 tablespoon caster sugar

2 teaspoons baking powder

1 cup (4oz) yellow polenta (cornmeal)

½ teaspoon salt

1 x 220g can sweet corn
(whole kernel corn), drained

½ cup grated cheddar cheese

1 tablespoon olive oil
(plus a little more for frying)

In a large bowl, combine eggs and milk. Whisk in the flour, sugar, baking powder, polenta and salt. Add corn, cheese and olive oil. Stir to combine.

Heat a little olive oil in a non-stick frypan.

Pour about ¼ of the pancake mixture into the pan.

Cook for 1–2 minutes, then turn the pancakes over and cook the other side for another 2 minutes.

CHEF'S NOTES:
Cornmeal pancakes make a great gluten-free breakfast! I like to serve these with a sliced tomato or apple for breakfast, or with a salad for lunch. Simple and quick to make using standard cupboard ingredients, you can have these on the table in less than 30 minutes.

Baking

Baking

Gluten Free Bread Recipe

INGREDIENTS

BASE

320ml (11fl oz) water

120ml (4fl oz) oil olive

3.5g (1/8oz) xanthan gum

80g (2½oz) rice flour

80g (2½oz) tapioca starch

90g (3oz) besan flour

5g (1/6oz) yeast

40ml (1 1/3fl oz) warm water

2g (1/5oz) caster sugar

SPECIAL EQUIPMENT:

Electric themometer

Preheat oven to 220°C (420°F/Gas Mark 7).

Heat water and oil together until mixture reaches 60°C (120°F). Remove from heat, slowly add the xanthan gum until it's thick and smooth. Continue mixing until mixture cools to room temperature.

In a large bowl, sift together rice flour, tapioca starch and besan flour. Add to water and oil mixture and stir until mixture forms a smooth batter.

Mix yeast with warm water and sugar; cover and allow to sit until mixture rises. Add to batter and mix until dough forms.

Mould required shape and leave to sit for a few hours until dough 'reproves' and doubles in size. This will help the bubbles grow in the bread. If you don't reprove the bread, it will become too dense. Cook bread in oven approximately 20–25 minutes, glazing with olive oil.

Short Crust Pastry

Makes enough for 3 tarts

INGREDIENTS

1½ cups gluten-free cornflour

½ cup soya flour

½ teaspoon salt

125g (4oz) butter or nuttelex

1 egg yolk

¼ cup water

To convert this to a sweet pastry, add 50g (1¾oz) caster sugar when sifting the flours.

Sift the cornflour, soya flour and salt into a bowl. Using fingertips, rub in butter until the mixture resembles fine breadcrumbs. Add egg yolk and water, a little at a time, until blended. Turn out onto floured board and knead thoroughly.

Refrigerate overnight or for at least two hours before using.

Chocolate Eclairs

INGREDIENTS

CHOUX PASTRY

60g (2oz) butter or nuttelex

1 cup water

125g (4oz) gluten-free plain flour

2g ($\frac{1}{100}$oz) xanthan gum

4 eggs, lightly beaten

CRÈME PATISSERIE

500ml (16fl oz) milk

40g (1¾oz) caster sugar

400ml (14fl oz) cream

3 egg yolks

50g (2oz) caster sugar, extra

40g (1¾oz) gluten-free cornflour

1 vanilla bean, whole

100g (3½oz) dark chocolate melts

Preheat oven to 220°C (420°F/Gas Mark 7).

Heat butter in a large saucepan until melted. Add water and bring to the boil. Remove from heat and whisk in flour. Add xanthan gum. Return to a low heat and cook, stirring vigorously for at least 4–5 minutes.

Remove from the heat and pour mixture into a blender or food processor. Blend mixture on a medium speed until it cools down. If you are not sure if it's cool enough, turn the machine off and place your finger into the mix; if it's too hot for your finger to stay in there for a few seconds, then it's too hot for the eggs.

Once mixture has cooled, add eggs, a little at a time, mixing between additions. Transfer mixture to a piping bag and pipe pastry into 12cm (4¾ins) lengths onto paper-lined baking trays.

Cook in oven for approximately 12–15 minutes, then reduce heat to 160°C (310°F/Gas Mark 2) and cook a further 10 minutes.

Turn off heat and leave éclair shells to cool in the oven.

To make crème pattiserie, bring milk and caster sugar to the boil in a large saucepan.

Meanwhile, whisk cream, egg yolks, extra caster sugar and cornflour together to make a smooth paste.

Once the milk has boiled, whisk in egg mixture, cook on moderate heat until smooth and thick. Set aside to cool until thickened. Transfer mixture to a piping bag.

To assemble éclairs, bring a pot of water to the boil, then turn heat off and place a firm-fitting bowl on top. Add chocolate melts and stir until chocolate is melted. Dip éclairs into the chocolate and allow them to harden. Then, using a sharp serrated knife, cut the top off the éclairs, pipe the crème patisserie on one half of the pastry and top with the other half.

CHEF'S NOTES:

The choux pastry mixture ideally should be made and used the same day. However, it will keep in an airtight container or disposable piping bag for 2–3 days.

Sundried Tomato Muffins

INGREDIENTS

125g (4oz) white rice flour

125g (4oz) gluten-free self-raising flour

75g (2½oz) corn flour

125g (4oz) unsalted butter, melted

1 lemon rind, grated

3 eggs

125g (4oz) Greek yoghurt

10 sundried tomatoes, sliced thinly

1 bunch chives, chopped finely

Preheat oven to 170ºC (330ºF/ Gas Mark 2–3). Grease 10 holes of a muffin tray with a little olive oil.

Sift white rice flour, self-raising flour and corn flour together. Combine butter and lemon rind; add to flour mixture.

Add eggs, one at a time, beating between additions. Add yoghurt and stir until combined. Stir in sundried tomatoes and chives.

Cook in oven for 10–15 minutes, or until an inserted metal skewer comes out clean.

Apple and Cinnamon Muffins

INGREDIENTS

125g (4oz) white rice flour

125g (4oz) gluten-free self-raising flour

75g (3oz) corn flour

1 teaspoon gluten-free baking powder

½ tablespoon bicarbonate of soda

½ tablespoon cinnamon powder

2 eggs

125g (4oz) unsalted butter

100ml (3fl oz) apple juice

1 teaspoon sugar, or artificial sweetener

1 green, bitter apple

1 lemon rind, grated

Preheat oven to 170°C (330°F/ Gas Mark 2–3). Grease 10 holes of a muffin tin with a little olive oil.

In a large mixing bowl, sift together white rice flour, self-raising flour, corn flour, baking powder, bicarbonate of soda, and cinnamon powder. Add eggs, one at a time, mixing between additions.

Combine butter, apple juice and sweetener in a medium saucepan. Cook, stirring, until heated through. Add warm liquid to flour and egg mix. Stir to combine.

Peel, core and dice apple. Place into a pot of cold water and bring to the boil. Strain apple pieces, discard liquid and stir apple into muffin mix. Spoon mix into prepared muffin tin and cook in oven for 10–15 minutes.

CHEF'S NOTES:
We add the apple right at the very end to retain its green colour—I'm not too fond of brown!

Banana Butterscotch Muffins
with homemade ice cream

INGREDIENTS

6 over-ripe bananas

500g (1lb) gluten-free plain flour

200g (6½oz) brown sugar

45g (1½oz) baking powder

12 eggs

500g (1lb) unsalted butter

150ml (5fl oz) rice milk

BUTTERSCOTCH SAUCE

500g (20oz) brown sugar

200 g (8oz) unsalted butter

500ml (17fl oz) full fat cream

GLUTEN-FREE VANILLA ICE CREAM

10 egg yolks

200g (6½oz) caster sugar

1L (32fl oz) full cream milk

1L (32fl oz) pure cream

1 vanilla bean, split

CHEF'S NOTES:

Only prepare the anglaise when you are to ready to use it, as the sugar is hydroscopic and will cook the egg mixture, if you leave it without stirring. These muffins are great to freeze for the kid's lunches or bake them in a cake tin for a special occasion.

If you wish to serve this recipe with the homemade ice cream, it's best to make the ice cream a day or two in advance and freeze until required.

Preheat oven to 160°C (320°F/ Gas Mark 2–3).

Dice 3 bananas and puree the rest. In a large bowl, sift together the gluten-free flour, brown sugar and baking powder. Add eggs, one at a time, with the butter and milk. Mix by hand, or with an electric mixer on a medium speed, until smooth. Add bananas and mix again. Spoon mixture into muffin tray and cook in oven for 12–15 minutes.

Meanwhile, make butterscotch sauce: bring sugar, butter and cream to the boil, then reduce heat and simmer for 20 minutes, until mixture achieves desired thickness.

To make the ice cream, make an 'anglaise' first by whisking together egg yolks and sugar (reserve a little sugar for the milk mixture) in a large bowl.

In a heavy-based pot or saucepan over medium heat, cook milk and cream. Just before it's about to boil, add reserved sugar to stop it from sticking on the bottom. When milk and cream has reached a temperature around 80°C, remove from heat and whisk in egg mixture until smooth.

Continue whisking until mixture turns thick, then cool further, over ice if necessary, and push through a fine sieve. Put mixture in an ice cream maker and churn, or, if you don't have an ice cream maker, a large container. If using a container, stir mixture every hour until creamy.

Serve muffins topped with butterscotch sauce and dollop ice cream on the side.

Biscuits and Crunchy Crumbles

Almond Biscotti

Before starting to make biscuits, ensure there is enough room in the refrigerator for mixture to rest. There are 2 stages that require resting—forming the dough and shaping the dough.

In a large mixing bowl, sift together baking powder, icing sugar, flour and almond or hazelnut meal. Add almonds and stir to combine. Add eggs and almond essence, a little bit at a time, until fully incorporated and mixture forms a dough. Wrap dough in cling wrap and refrigerate for 10 minutes.

Preheat oven to 160°C (320°F/Gas Mark 2–3).

Put a little water on your hands to make it easier to shape the dough. Mould dough into log or slice into disc shapes and chill the re-shaped mixture again for about 10 minutes.

Brush biscuits will a little egg white before cooking to glaze. Cook in oven, 8 minutes or until golden brown.

Slice the cooked biscuits into thin slices and dry them out by re baking them in the oven. Once they have hardened, they are ready for eating.

INGREDIENTS

1 teaspoon gluten-free baking powder

170g (6oz) pure icing sugar

280g (9oz) gluten-free plain flour

100g (4oz) almond meal or hazelnut meal

20g (2/3oz) whole almonds,
blanched and toasted

2 eggs, lightly beaten

1/4 teaspoon almond essence

1 egg white, extra

CHEF'S NOTES:

I first learnt about Italian cuisine when working at The Point in Albert Park, back when it first opened. My Italian friends would often dip their dry biscotti into a Vino Santo dessert wine, yum! You could also have them with a dip or enjoy them with an espresso coffee. In this recipe, the resting stages are very important. The dough requires enough time to cool, otherwise it's bound to spread when cooking!

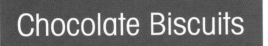
Chocolate Biscuits

INGREDIENTS

80g (2½oz) unsalted butter, softened

125g (4oz) caster sugar

125g (4oz) white rice flour

125g (4oz) Dutch cocoa powder

125g (4oz) cornflour

125g (4oz) gluten-free plain flour

2 eggs, beaten lightly

Milk chocolate chips, to decorate

50ml (2fl oz) water

Preheat oven to 180°C (350°F/Gas Mark 4).

Combine butter and caster sugar. You can do this by using a paddle attachment on your mixer or by hand with a wooden spoon. Sift in rice flour, cocoa powder, cornflour and plain flour and combine slowly, using a wooden spoon.

Add eggs and mix smooth. The mixture does not need to be over-worked like bread, as it has a different texture and will rise with the help of the eggs.

Once smooth, roll mixture into balls and place on a greased baking tray. Squash mixture balls down with a spoon or fork. Stud the biscuits with chocolate chips and cook in oven for 15 minutes. Leave to cool on a wire rack or just eat them like I would, while they are nice and warm—yum!

Lemon Tea-time

INGREDIENTS

120g (4oz) butter or nuttelex

100g (3½oz) caster sugar

210g (7oz) gluten-free self-raising flour

10g (⅓oz) cornflour

3g (⅕oz) xanthan gum

3g (⅕oz) guar gum

½ vanilla bean, split, seeds scraped out

50ml (1¾fl oz) lemon juice

½ lemon rind, grated finely

Preheat oven to 160ºC (320ºF/Gas Mark 2–3).

Beat butter and sugar with an electric mixer until pale. Sift in self-raising flour, cornflour, gums and vanilla. Mix on medium speed. Add lemon juice and zest, mix until smooth.

On a piece of silicon paper, roll out the biscuit dough and cut with a round or scalloped edge cutter. Place biscuits onto a baking tray and rest in the fridge for about 15 minutes. Cook in oven about 12–15 minutes, or until golden brown.

Allow to rest on the tray for about 5 minutes before turning them onto a wire rack to cool.

CHEF'S NOTES:

Store these yummy biscuits in an airtight container, if they last that long...

Anzac Biscuits

INGREDIENTS

5g (1/6oz) bicarbonate of soda

60ml (2fl oz) boiling water

170g (6oz) butter or nuttelex

50g (2oz) golden syrup

250g (8oz) puffed rice

200g (6½oz) gluten-free oats

100g (3½oz) desiccated coconut

220g (7oz) gluten-free plain flour, sifted

Preheat oven to 160°C (320°F/Gas Mark 2–3). Line 2 large oven trays with baking paper.

In a small bowl, combine bicarbonate of soda and water.

In a small heavy-based saucepan, combine butter and golden syrup. Cook over a low heat until melted, then add the bicarbonate soda mixture. Increase the heat and stir to combine.

In a large mixing bowl, combine puffed rice, oats, coconut and flour. Make a well in the centre and pour in the butter mixture. Stir until well combined and moist.

Divide mixture into approximately 20 balls or tablespoons and press onto lined baking trays. Leave plenty of space between biscuits to allow for them spreading. Bake for 12–15 minutes or until golden.

Stand trays on wire racks until the biscuits are firm and cool, then transfer biscuits to wire racks and leave until cold.

CHEF'S NOTES:

Who says we need to miss out on great Australian snacks like the Aussie Anzac Biscuit? Gluten-free food is limitless in my eyes—try this recipe and you'll never look back! Anzac biscuits can be stored in an airtight container, refrigerated, up to 7 days.

INGREDIENTS

150g (5oz) butter or nuttelex

80ml (2¾fl oz) coconut cream

225g (7¼oz) caster sugar

50g (1¾oz) organic honey

120g (4oz) flaked almonds

120g (4oz) whole almonds, coarsely chopped

40g (1¼oz) glacé red cherries, coarsely chopped

50g (1¾oz) blackcurrants

15g (½oz) glacé ginger

Preheat oven to 160°C (320°F/Gas Mark 2–3).

Heat butter in a large pot or saucepan. Add coconut cream and sugar. Bring to the boil then reduce heat and simmer for 5 minutes.

Add remaining ingredients and cook for a further 2 minutes on high heat, stirring continuously to prevent any of the ingredients sticking.

When mixture has a dough-like consistency, transfer to a bowl and cool slightly (not too much otherwise it will harden).

I usually bake my biscuit mix in muffin tins, to keep uniform height and shape, but it's up to you!

Cook florentines on the top shelves of the oven for 10–12 minutes.

CHEF'S NOTES:

If you're not sure what they should look like when they're cooked, go with your nose. Like all baking, you should smell a beautiful aroma around your house when it's cooked. When removing from the oven, allow to cool. You could dip them in some melted chocolate to jazz them up if you like.

Butterscotch Shortbread

INGREDIENTS

200g (6½ oz) butter or nuttelex

1 teaspoon vanilla essence

75g (2½oz) brown sugar

260g (8½oz) gluten-free plain flour

1 teaspoon guar gum

1 teaspoon xanthan gum

BUTTERSCOTCH FILLING

120g (3¾oz) icing sugar

50g (2oz) brown sugar

75g (3oz) butter or nuttelex

½ vanilla bean, split, seeds scraped out

Preheat oven to 160°C (320°F/Gas Mark 2–3).

Beat butter, vanilla essence and sugar with an electric mixer on high speed for about 2 minutes. (Ideally, you should use an electric mixing bowl with paddle attachment).

In a separate bowl, sift together remaining dry ingredients and stir to combine. Add to butter mixture and beat on high speed until smooth.

Roll the dough into a cylinder shape and wrap in cling wrap if you wish to keep it a uniform shape. Refrigerate until required.

Cut the biscuits to about 1cm (½in) thick. If they are too thick, they won't cook evenly.

Cook in oven approximately 8–10 minutes. Check that the dough is not becoming too dark as it will turn the shortbreads bitter.

Remove from oven and set aside to cool.

Meanwhile, make the filling by sifting the icing sugar into a bowl, then using an electric mixer, combine sugar with remaining icing ingredients and beating until smooth.

To serve, spread a generous layer of butterscotch filling between 2 shortbread fingers. Enjoy with morning tea, afternoon tea or anything in between!

CHEF'S NOTES:
The biscuit dough will keep for weeks refrigerated in an airtight container, or make it in bulk and freeze.

Puddings and Mousses

Strawberry Mousse
with citrus salad and berry sorbet

CHEF'S NOTES:

Inverted sugar, once cooled, can be kept in an airtight container for at least 4–6 months. This product is really easy to use and it will give your chocolate work and ice creams another dimension in stability. If blood orange puree is not in season you could use orange juice with a touch of grenadine. If you're confident with making sorbets, use 3 ladles of liquid nitrogen and whisk into the mixture, then freeze.

Serves 10

INGREDIENTS

1kg (2lb) caster sugar

500ml (16fl oz) water

¼ teaspoon cream of tartar or citric acid

1L (32fl oz) blood orange puree

1kg (2lb) strawberries, pureed

4 sheets gelatine

1L (32fl oz) semi-whipped cream

BERRY SORBET

1kg (2lb) blueberries frozen

1kg (2lb) raspberries frozen

1kg (2lb) strawberries frozen

1kg (2lb) blackberries frozen

CITRUS SALAD

10 oranges

20 strawberries

100ml (4fl oz) fruit coulis [Refer to Chocolate tian recipe, page 75]

1 bunch mint leaves

SPECIAL EQUIPMENT

Electronic Thermometer

In a saucepan, combine caster sugar, water and cream of tartar. Do not stir this mixture! Bring to the boil until it reaches 114°C (250°F). Remove from heat and set aside to cool. This is known as 'inverted sugar' and we will use this throughout the recipe.

Boil orange puree with 500ml (16fl oz) of the inverted sugar, without stirring, until mixture reaches 114°C (250°F). Remove from heat, pour into moulds and freeze.

To make the strawberry mousse, in a large saucepan, heat a little strawberry puree on low heat. Add gelatine and stir until it dissolves. Add remaining puree. Take mixture off the heat and allow to cool. Once it's almost cold, fold in the semi-whipped cream.

Half-fill serving dishes with mousse mixture and allow to set. Add about 1 teaspoon of the frozen orange mixture per dish, then freeze again until set. Once set, top with remaining mousse. Cover and freeze until required.

To make the berry sorbet, defrost all berries. Using a stick blender, puree until smooth. Push berry mixture through a sieve and reserve liquid and pulp.

Make a syrup by using 1 part inverted sugar to 4 parts fruit pulp. Add half the liquid from the sorbet syrup. Freeze sorbet mixture or use a domestic ice cream churner.

To make the citrus salad, peel oranges and remove the white pith. You can do this by cutting the outer part of the skin off the orange by following the shape of the orange. Coat orange and strawberry segments with coulis.

Serve mousse with sorbet and citrus salad, garnished with mint leaves.

Fig and Ricotta Bread Pudding

INGREDIENTS

15 whole fresh figs or green dry variety figs

50g (2oz) caster sugar

50ml (2fl oz) frangelico (optional)

300ml (10fl oz) cream

40g (1¾oz) caster sugar (or equivalent artificial sweetener), extra

3 eggs, lightly beaten

200ml (7fl oz) soy or rice milk

1 whole vanilla bean, split

100g (3½oz) ricotta

10 slices gluten-free bread, cut into triangles

50g (2oz) butter or nuttelex

1 cinnamon stick, toasted and crushed

Preheat oven to 160°C (310°F/Gas Mark 2–3).

If the figs you've bought are dried, re-hydrate them by placing in a deep ovenproof tray with the sugar and enough water to half-cover them. Cook in oven until soft (approximately 15 minutes). Remove from oven and add a dash of Frangelico, if desired. They taste really good so make sure there's some left for the pudding!

Slice figs to 5cm (2ins) thick. In a large mixing bowl, combine cream, sugar and eggs. This will dissolve the sugar. Heat milk and add the vanilla bean to it. Sprinkle with a little sugar to stop the lactose catching on the bottom. Crumble in ricotta. Add to the cream mixture and mix well.

Layer gluten-free bread triangles in a greased ovenproof dish and top with some of the figs. Pour some of the cream mixture over the top and continue layering until all the bread is gone. Crush cinnamon in a mortar and pestle until flaky and soft. Sprinkle cinnamon over pudding.

Cook pudding at 165°C (325°F/Gas Mark 2–3) for 10-12 minutes or until the liquid has set. Serve pudding warm or chilled, with fresh fruit or straight out of the dish.

CHEF'S NOTES:
The liquid is a royal-style mixture which contains eggs, so it's important not to overheat it too much or the eggs will curdle! The egg mixture should set solid, like a custard tart.

Date and Banana Pudding
with butterscotch sauce

INGREDIENTS

300g (10oz) fresh or dried dates

200ml (6fl oz) water

2½g (¹/₁₀oz) xanthan gum

5g (¹/₅oz) bicarbonate of soda

1 vanilla bean, split and seeds scraped

3 overripe bananas

200g (6½oz) butter or nuttelex

150g (5oz) brown sugar

8 eggs

300g (9½oz) gluten-free self-raising flour

BUTTERSCOTCH SAUCE

200g (7oz) organic brown sugar

100g (4oz) nuttelex

1 vanilla bean, split

200 ml (7fl.oz) full fat cream

CHEF'S NOTES:

You can test if the puddings are done by inserting a metal skewer into the centre, if your skewer comes out clean, the pudding's ready. However, most cakes or pastries will let you know when they're cooked by sending out their amazing aromas!

In a saucepan, cover dates with cold water and bring to the boil. Remove dates from liquid and set aside to cool. Whisk xanthan gum into water, over a medium heat, until thick and smooth. Set aside.

Using a potato masher, crush dates together with bicarbonate of soda and vanilla bean seeds. Adding the bicarbonate soda helps the dates break down, releases the pigments and increases the colour.

Once dates are soft, add the thickened liquid and bananas.

Preheat oven to 160ºC (310ºF/Gas Mark 2–3).

Cream the butter and sugar together until pale. Add one egg at a time, then sift in flour. Use an electric mixer to beat until fully combined. Add date and banana mixture.

Grease serving moulds with butter and sugar on the inside, or spray silicon moulds with oil. Cook puddings in oven for 10 minutes.

To make butterscotch sauce, combine all sauce ingredients in a large saucepan and bring to the boil. Stirring until sauce thickens and coats the back of the spoon.

Turn out puddings (or keep them in mould) then saturate in the butterscotch sauce. Add a little extra sauce around the outside of the plate to decorate and serve with ice cream, if desired.

Steamed Blood Orange Pudding

INGREDIENTS

6 blood oranges

500g (1lb) gluten-free plain flour

1 teaspoon baking powder

280g (9oz) butter or nuttelex

1 vanilla bean, split

250g (8oz) caster sugar

6 eggs, lightly beaten

220ml (6fl oz) milk

Cut oranges in half and juice all the liquid from them. Reserve juice and grate the rind. Set aside until required.

In a medium bowl, sift flour and baking powder together. In a separate bowl, beat butter, vanilla bean and sugar with an electric beater, until pale. Add a little of the egg, a little flour mixture and a little milk, alternating until finished. This process allows for the butter to re-emulsify after each egg. Stir in orange rind.

Grease small ceramic bowls or coffee cups and sprinkle the inside with sugar. This will help stop them sticking and help to caramelise your pudding. Spoon pudding mixture into each cup, only filling it half way up—the puddings need to rise.

Using a vegetable steamer, cook puddings for 18 minutes on a medium heat. Puddings need to be cooked solid all the way through.

Pour blood orange juice over puddings and serve.

INGREDIENTS

1kg (2lb) mixed, dried fruit, 'fructose friendly'

1 tablespoon Amaretto liqueur (optional)

1 tablespoon Cointreau (optional)

125g (4oz) butter

1 teaspoon mixed spice

1 teaspoon nutmeg

4 eggs, lightly beaten

1 tablespoon Parisian essence (brown food colouring, optional)

440g (14oz) canned unsweetened pineapple, crushed

125g (4oz) almonds

1 teaspoon pre-gel starch (or xanthan/guar gum)

1 teaspoon cream of tartar

1 teaspoon bicarbonate of soda

1 cup gluten-free flour

Preheat oven to 140°C (275°F/Gas Mark 2). Line a log dish with baking paper.

In a large saucepan, cook the dried fruit (and liqueurs, if using) on a high heat for five minutes. Add the butter, mixed spices and nutmeg. Transfer to a large bowl and stir in remaining ingredients.

Spread mixture evenly into log dish. Cook, elevated, in oven for 15 minutes (for example, on a small upturned dish). Test cake with a skewer; when it comes out clean, the cake is ready.

Remove from oven and allow the cake to cool before removing from the container.

CHEF'S NOTES:

This could be the easiest Christmas cake ever! It can be stored, refrigerated, for a few days. The flavours meld together and the taste actually improves after a few days. You could make your own gluten-free flour mix by combining ½ cup soya flour, ¼ cup rice flour and ¼ cup potato flour.

Steamed Saucy Chocolate Puddings

CHEF'S NOTES:

When using a microwave to melt chocolate, keep a close eye on it to avoid burning. Stir with a metal spoon every minute until the chocolate almost melts. Then remove and stir, until it's fully melted and smooth. If you're too nervous using the microwave, you can always use your stove top, placing a bowl over a pot of boiling water and mixing continuously.

Serves 8

INGREDIENTS

25g (1oz) melted butter, to grease

25g (1oz) gluten-free plain flour, to dust moulds

150g (5oz) butter, at room temperature, chopped

120g (4oz) lightly packed brown sugar

1 teaspoon vanilla essence

2 eggs, lightly whisked

100g (3½oz) dark chocolate, coarsely chopped

115g (3¾oz) gluten-free, self-raising flour

40g (1½oz) gluten-free plain flour, extra

30g (1oz) cocoa powder

80ml (2¾fl oz) milk

CHOCOLATE FUDGE SAUCE

100g (3½oz) dark chocolate, coarsely chopped

60g (2oz) lightly packed brown sugar

2 tablespoons cocoa powder, sifted

250ml (8fl oz) thickened cream

Grease 8 cups or small bowls with butter. Dust with flour and line the bases with non-stick baking paper.

Using an electric beater, beat butter, sugar and vanilla for 8 minutes or until your mixture is pale and creamy. Add half the egg to the butter mixture and beat to combine, then add the remaining egg and beat until smooth.

Melt chocolate in a small, microwave-safe bowl by heating it in the microwave on a medium/500watts/50% heat for 1 minute at a time, stirring between minutes until chocolate has almost melted. Remove and stir until chocolate melts fully and is smooth. Add to butter mixture and beat to combine.

In a separate bowl, sift the gluten-free flour and cocoa powder together. Add half of this flour mixture and half the milk to chocolate mixture. Using wooden spoon or spatula, stir until well combined. Repeat with the remaining flour mixture and milk. Spoon chocolate mixture into prepared cups or bowls.

In the base of a large saucepan with a tight-fitting lid, fit a small rack or upturned heatproof saucer. Place as many cups as you can fit in the saucepan. Add enough boiling water to reach two-thirds of the way up the side of the cups. Cover and bring to a simmer over medium heat. Cook, covered, for 20 minutes or until a skewer inserted into the centre of the puddings comes out clean. Cover and set aside 10 minutes to cool slightly. Turn onto a serving plate.

To make the chocolate fudge sauce, combine chocolate, brown sugar, cocoa powder and cream in a small saucepan over a low heat until mixture resembles thickened cream. Set aside for 2 minutes, then stir until the chocolate has melted and the mixture is smooth.

Serve chocolate puddings sliced into wedges and covered with the chocolate fudge sauce. Add fresh strawberries and ice cream, if desired. Wow!

Chocolate Fondant
with strawberries and cream

INGREDIENTS

50g (2oz) caster sugar (to sprinkle in moulds)

½ punnet strawberries (about 150g or 5oz), cleaned, hulled and sliced thinly

5g (⅙oz) cracked black pepper

140g (4½oz) caster sugar, extra

50g (2oz) milk chocolate

50g (2oz) unsalted butter

1 egg, beaten lightly

20g (⅔oz) gluten-free self-raising flour

50g (2oz) double cream

Preheat oven to 185ºC (350ºF/Gas mark 4). Grease fondant moulds with butter and sprinkle a little sugar to stop mixture from sticking.

In a large pot, combine strawberries with pepper and sugar. Add enough water to cover, bring mixture to a boil, then remove from heat and place in a bowl to marinate until required.

In a large, heatproof bowl set over a pot of boiling water, combine chocolate, butter and sugar. Stir mixture until smooth. Remove from heat and slowly add the egg, mixing together with a spoon, until the mixture becomes syrupy.

Add flour and stir until smooth. Fill fondant moulds to ¾ full. Cook in oven for 10 minutes until semi-set. Serve fondants with peppered strawberries topped with double cream.

Tarts and Tortes

Pear and Almond Frangipani Tart

INGREDIENTS

450g (14oz) unsalted butter

250g (8oz) pure icing sugar

1 vanilla bean, split

3 eggs, beaten lightly

100g (3½oz) almond meal

750g (1½lb) gluten-free plain flour

Salt

100g (3½oz) sweet pastry

4 fresh pears, peeled, cored and sliced into thin wedges

200g (6½oz) raspberries

100g (3½oz) flaked almonds

50g (1²⁄₃oz) pure icing sugar

Preheat oven to 170°C (325°F/Gas Mark 2–3).

To make the frangipani mixture, use an electric mixer to beat butter, sugar and vanilla together. Add the eggs, one at a time, beating between additions. Sift in almond meal and plain flour and salt and knead until smooth. Do not overwork. Flatten, wrap in cling wrap and refrigerate for 30 minutes.

Roll out sweet pastry and use it to line a lightly floured tart mould.

Use a piping bag to control the frangipani mixture and spread it into the prepared mould. Press pear wedges onto mixture in circular pattern. Place raspberries evenly into spaces between pears. Sprinkle with flaked almonds, dust with icing sugar and cook in oven until pastry is golden brown.

Lemon Tart

INGREDIENTS

225g (7oz) butter

450g (15oz) gluten-free plain flour

225g (7oz) caster sugar

2 eggs, beaten lightly

1 lemon rind, grated finely

LEMON CREAM

12 egg yolks

300g (10oz) caster sugar

125g (4oz) gluten-free corn flour

1L (32fl oz) milk

2 lemons, juiced, rind removed and grated finely

500ml (16fl oz) cream

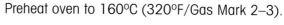

Preheat oven to 160°C (320°F/Gas Mark 2–3).

To make the pastry, combine butter and flour in a medium bowl. Using fingertips, rub the butter and the flour together until mixture resembles breadcrumbs. Add sugar. Fold eggs into the mix with lemon rind. Stir to combine but do not over mix. Set aside for 10 minutes.

To make the lemon cream, in a separate bowl whisk yolks and sugar together until sugar begins to dissolve. Add flour and stir to combine. In a small saucepan on low heat, heat milk until warm. Add flour mixture and stir until thick. Add lemon zest and lemon juice and stir to combine. Remove from heat and set aside to cool. Whip cream and fold into lemon mixture.

Roll out pastry to about 5mm ($^{1}/_{5}$in) thick and line tart moulds. Bake tart cases, filled with baking beans, raw rice or baking weights (this is known as blind baking), in oven for 15 minutes or until cases are lightly coloured and cooked on the bottom.

Remove from oven and set aside to cool. Fill pastry with lemon cream, and allow to set before cutting.

Dust with icing sugar to serve or caramelise with a blowtorch to give it a crisp top.

Pecan and Mascarpone Torte

INGREDIENTS

150g (5oz) flaked or whole almonds, toasted

150g (5oz) pecans

300g (10oz) dark chocolate

40ml (1 ¼fl oz) brandy

150g (5oz) unsalted butter, softened

150g (5oz) caster sugar

4 eggs, lightly beaten

1 vanilla bean, split

200g (6½oz) mascarpone

Preheat oven to 170°C (325°F/Gas mark 2–3). Grease a 23cm (9ins) springform tin with a little olive oil.

Whiz nuts in a food processor or blender until they resemble coarse breadcrumbs. Sprinkle some of the nut mixture into the tin and spread around to coat bottom and sides. Reserve remaining nut mixture.

In a heatproof bowl over a saucepan of simmering water, combine chocolate and brandy and cook, stirring occasionally until chocolate is melted. Set aside to cool slightly.

Whiz butter and sugar in food processor or blender until pale. Transfer to a large bowl. Add the remaining nut mixture, melted chocolate mixture, eggs, vanilla and mascarpone. Mix well and pour mixture into prepared tin.

Cook in oven for 50–60 minutes or until just set. Remove from oven and leave to rest in the tin about 15 minutes before removing. Serve torte dusted with a little cocoa powder, if desired.

Apple and Rhubarb Crumble

INGREDIENTS

2 bunches rhubarb, peeled if necessary and chopped into 5cm (2ins) sticks

8 Granny Smith apples, peeled, cored and chopped into 3cm (1¼ins) cubes

100g (3½oz) caster sugar

400g (13oz) gluten-free plain flour

500g (1lb) caster sugar, extra

4 teaspoons ground cinnamon

600g (1¼lb) unsalted butter

200ml (6½fl oz) double cream

Preheat oven to 180ºC (350ºF/Gas Mark 4).

Combine rhubarb, apples and sugar in a large pot. Cover with water and bring to the boil. Reduce heat and cook until fruit is tender. Remove from heat, set aside to cool then drain. Divide fruit mixture among serving dishes.

Meanwhile, combine flour, sugar and cinnamon in a large bowl.

Using fingertips, rub in the butter until mixture resembles breadcrumbs. Spread mixture onto a greased baking tray and cook for 2 minutes until golden brown.

Cover fruit with crumble mix and reheat in oven for 5 minutes just before serving. Serve crumble with double cream.

chutneys
and
Pickles

Jars

Using Jars

Use jars that are free from cracks, chips or flaws. The best sizes to use are 450g (1lb), although 1kg (2lb) jars can be used for pickling fruit.

Prepare the jars by washing well in warm, soapy water and rinsing thoroughly. Dry the jars in an oven set at 140°C (275°F/Gas Mark 2). Fill jars with chutney or pickle while they are still warm, to prevent the jars from cracking. Fill to within 1cm ($\frac{1}{2}$ inch) of the top. Cover with a waxed disc (wax side down) and immediately place a cellophane disc over the top. Cover with a screw-top lid.

Fig Chutney

INGREDIENTS

1 apple, peeled, cored and finely chopped

½ teaspoon salt

125g (4oz) ripe tomatoes, peeled, deseeded and coarsely chopped

60g (2oz) onion (approximately 1 onion), finely chopped

60g (2oz) sultanas

1 tablespoon orange rind, chopped roughly

1 orange, juiced

150g (5oz) caster sugar

¼ teaspoon ground cinnamon

¼ teaspoon ground nutmeg

¼ teaspoon cayenne pepper

15g (½ oz) fresh ginger, finely chopped

150ml (5fl oz) white wine vinegar

Pinch saffron powder

375g (13oz) fresh figs, finely chopped

Combine all ingredients except figs in a heavy-based saucepan on low heat.

Bring to the boil, stirring occasionally with a wooden spoon.

Reduce heat and simmer for approximately 1 hour, stirring every 10 minutes, until the mixture is jam-like and syrupy. Add the figs and cook on very low heat, stirring every 10 minutes, a further 40 minutes.

Remove from heat and set aside to cool. Once cooled, transfer to prepared jars.

CHEF'S NOTES:
To peel tomatoes, bring a pot of water to the boil and gently drop the whole tomatoes in. Leave a minute or two, until they start to split, then remove from water with a slotted spoon and drop into a bowl of cold water. The skins should have split and you should then be able to peel them. Cut in half, deseed and then chop.

Date Chutney

INGREDIENTS

1$\frac{1}{3}$kg (2lb10oz) dates, pitted and roughly chopped

450g (15oz) spring onions, white parts only, sliced thinly

225g (8oz) raisins

100g (3$\frac{1}{2}$oz) currants

225g (7oz) sugar

50g (2oz) salt

25g (1oz) allspice

12g ($\frac{1}{2}$oz) mustard seed

1$\frac{1}{10}$L (35fl oz) white wine vinegar

Combine all ingredients in a heavy-based saucepan on low heat. Bring to the boil, stirring occasionally with a wooden spoon. Reduce heat and simmer, stirring occasionally, until mixture is soft and thick.

Transfer to prepared jars and store in a cool dark place for 2–3 months before consuming.

Tomato Chutney

INGREDIENTS

24 tomatoes, coarsely chopped

8 onions, coarsely chopped

2 cucumbers, coarsely chopped

30g (1oz) salt

1kg (2lb) caster sugar

1L (32fl oz) white wine vinegar

60ml (2fl oz) Dijon mustard

2 tablespoons gluten-free curry powder

1 teaspoon cayenne pepper

1teaspoon gluten-free plain flour

In a large bowl, combine tomatoes, onions, cucumbers and salt. Cover and refrigerate overnight to marinate.

Drain, discard liquid and transfer tomato mixture to large saucepan.

Add sugar and vinegar, bring to the boil, then continue to boil until mixture is tender. Reduce heat and simmer. Add mustard, curry powder and cayenne pepper, then sprinkle in the flour. Continue to simmer, adding a little more vinegar if necessary, until the vegetables are tender.

Transfer to prepared jar. Tomato chutney can be used immediately.

Mango Chutney

Makes approximately 660g (22oz)

INGREDIENTS

1kg (2lb) mango, peeled and quartered

675g (1¼lb) apples, peeled and coarsely chopped

100g (3½oz) dates, pitted

50g (2oz) sultanas

50g (2oz) onion (approximately 1 onion)

25g (¾oz) salt

1 lemon, juiced

1 teaspoon cayenne pepper

¼ teaspoon nutmeg

3 bay leaves

600ml (18fl oz) brown vinegar

1kg (2lb) sugar

½ lime, juiced

In a large bowl, combine all ingredients except sugar and lime juice. Mix well and set aside to marinate at least 3 hours. Transfer to a large saucepan over medium heat and bring to the boil. Reduce heat and simmer until fruits are tender, stirring constantly.

Add the sugar and lime juice then continue to simmer until mixture thickens.

Spoon the hot mixture into warmed jars, cover, seal, and label and store in a cool dark place for 2–3 months before consuming.

Korean Cucumber Kimchi

Makes approximately 660g (22oz)

INGREDIENTS

450g (15oz) Lebanese cucumbers

30g (1oz) salt

100g (3½oz) white radish, julienned

50g (2oz) leeks, julienned

1 teaspoon crushed garlic

50g ginger, grated

½–1 tablespoon chilli powder, depending on taste

1 teaspoon sugar

1 tablespoon anchovy sauce

Slice cucumbers in half lengthways, then cut into slices about 1cm (½ inch) thick. In a colander, sprinkle cucumber with salt and set aside for about 30 minutes.

Meanwhile, combine radish, leeks, garlic, ginger, chilli, sugar, and anchovy sauce in a large bowl and mix well. Set aside for 20 minutes to marinate.

Drain cucumbers, removing as much moisture as possible, then add to the radish mixture and mix well. Cover with cling wrap and leave at room temperature for 24 hours. Transfer to prepared jars and chill before using.

Mustard Pickle

INGREDIENTS

50g (2oz) caster sugar

25g (1oz) salt

1¾L (52fl oz) white wine vinegar

50g (2oz) Dijon mustard

50g (2oz) mustard seeds

225g (7oz) carrots, chopped coarsely

1 medium cauliflower, cut into 3cm (1in) pieces

450g (15oz) cucumber, chopped coarsely

450g (15oz) brown onions, chopped coarsely

In a large saucepan, combine sugar, salt and vinegar. Bring to the boil.

Whisk in the mustard and mustard seeds, then add the carrots and cauliflower and boil for 15 minutes. Add the remaining vegetables and cook until vegetables are tender.

Spoon the hot mixture into prepared jars. Store in a cool dark place for 2–3 months before consuming.

Preserved Lemons

INGREDIENTS

24 lemons

70g (2½oz) honey

250ml (8fl oz) lemon juice

750ml (24fl oz) water

350g (11½oz) salt

1 tablespoon coriander seeds

2 cinnamon sticks

2 star anise

Score lemons and freeze overnight so they are really hard. In a medium saucepan, bring the honey, lemon juice and water to the boil. Without defrosting lemons, transfer them to prepared jars and pour water mixture over the lemons.

Add salt, coriander seeds, cinnamon sticks and star anise. Store in a cool dark place for 14 days before consuming.

Pepper Chutney

INGREDIENTS

6 red capsicums (peppers), seeded and diced

4 yellow capsicums (peppers), seeded and diced

1 onion, diced

2 cloves garlic, peeled and chopped finely

100ml (3fl oz) white wine vinegar

80g (2½oz) brown sugar

300g (10oz) tomato paste

1L (32fl oz) vegetable stock

Bouquet garni (a mixture of dried herbs, eg thyme, parsley, bay leaf)

Salt and pepper

Heat a little olive oil in a frypan.

Add capsicums, onions and garlic, and cook 3 minutes or until onions are translucent.

Add vinegar and cook until mixture reduces, and all the liquid evaporates.

Add brown sugar and caramelise slightly, then add the tomato paste and cook until mixture looks oily.

Add vegetable stock and bring mixture to the boil. Add the bouquet garni, season with salt and pepper.

Reduce heat and simmer for 5 minutes, adding more water if required.

Simmer until peppers are soft, then remove from heat and transfer to prepared jars.

Glossary of Terms

Bomba Rice: A short grain rice grown in Calasparra, Spain. The basic difference between Bomba rice and others is that Bomba expands in width rather than length. It differs from Italian Arborio rice, which is creamy, and Asian rice, which is sticky. Bomba absorbs three times its volume in liquid, yet the grains remain distinct. When you are making paella, this is just what you want to bring uniform flavor to your creation

Buckwheat Polenta: In the Italian Alps, where it's too cold to grow corn, buckwheat thrives and so black or buckwheat polenta became a popular peasant dish. It has lots of energy and a marbled appearance.

Cardamom: True cardamom has large leaves and white flowers with blue stripes and yellow borders. The tree grows to about 3m (10 ft) in height. The fruit is a small capsule with 8 to 16 brown seeds. The seeds are used as a spice.

Couverture Chocolate: In order to be properly labeled as 'couverture', chocolate must contain 32–39 per cent cocoa butter and the total of the percentage of the combined cocoa butter plus cocoa solids must be at least 54%. The higher percentage of cocoa butter, combined with the processing, gives the chocolate more sheen, firmer 'snap' when broken, and a creamy flavour. Do not substitute couverture for semi-sweet, bittersweet, or unsweetened chocolate as it may alter the finished product.

Caramelisation: is the oxidation of sugar, resulting in a nutty flavor and brown colour.

Crème Patisserie: While 'custard' may refer to a wide variety of thickened dishes, technically (and in French cookery) the word custard refers only to an egg-thickened custard. When starch is added, the result is called pastry cream (crème pâtissière), which is made with a combination of milk or cream, egg yolks, fine sugar, flour or some other starch, and usually a flavoring such as vanilla, chocolate, or lemon.

Garam Masala: From Hindi garam ('hot') and masala ('mixture'), garam masala is a basic blend of ground spices common in Indian and other South Asian cuisines. It is used alone or with other seasonings. The word garam refers to spice intensity, not heat. The composition of garam masala differs regionally. Some common ingredients are peppercorns, cloves, bay leaves, cumin seeds, cinnamon; black, brown and green cardamom, nutmeg, star anise and coriander seeds.

Ganache: This is said to have first been used around 1850 in Switzerland or France. Ganache is normally made by heating heavy/double cream, then pouring it over chopped dark chocolate. Depending on the kind of chocolate used, what the ganache is intended for, and the temperature it will be served at, the ratio of chocolate to cream can be varied to obtain the desired consistency.

Gremolata: A chopped herb condiment typically made of garlic, parsley, and lemon zest.

Mungbean Noodles: Mung bean starch, which is extracted from ground mung beans, is used to make transparent cellophane noodles (also known as bean thread noodles, bean thread and glass noodles)

Mirexpoix: Mirepoix is a combination of celery, carrot and onion. This 'holy trinity' is an essential ingredient in dozens, if not hundreds, of traditional French dishes. When dicing the separate ingredients, try to make the dices as small and uniform as possible, both because it is aesthetically more pleasing and because the small pieces will cook more uniformly.

Madeira: A fortified Portuguese wine made in the Madeira Islands. The wine is produced in a variety of styles ranging from dry wines which can be consumed on their own as an aperitif, to sweet wines more usually consumed with dessert.

Palliard: A thin slice of meat, grilled or sautéed.

Prosciutto: A dry-cured ham that is usually sliced thinly and served uncooked; this style is called prosciutto crudo in Italian. Commonly associated with Tuscany and Emilia, the most renowned and expensive legs of prosciutto come from central and northern Italy, such as those of Parma, Friuli-Venezia Giulia, and San Daniele.

Quinoa: Pronounced keen-wa, this is a species of goosefoot (Chenopodium), grown primarily for its edible seeds. It is a pseudo-cereal rather than a true cereal, or grain. A common cooking method is to treat quinoa like rice, bringing two cups of water to a boil with one cup of grain, covering at a low simmer and cooking for 14–18 minutes or until the germ separates from the seed. The cooked germ looks like a tiny curl and should have a slight bite to it (like al dente pasta).

Spätzle A type of noodle-pasta. In Europe, spätzle are considered a speciality of the Swabish area of Germany—the states of Baden-Württemberg and Bavaria.

Soufflé A light, fluffy, baked cake made with egg yolks and beaten egg whites combined with various other ingredients and served as a savory main dish or sweetened as a dessert.

Tarte Tatin An upside-down apple tart in which the apples are caramelised in butter and sugar before the tart is baked.

Turmeric is part of the ginger family, native to tropical South Asia. It has become the key ingredient for many Indian, Persian, Thai and Malay dishes.

Tuille biscuit A light wafer like pastry, used for desserts and also savory dishes. Commonly used as a crisp alongside something soft. The Tuille will give any dish a great dimension to the eating.

Wombok Also known as Chinese cabbage, celery cabbage, Tientsin cabbage and wong nga bok, womboks remain one of the most popular vegetables in Asia. The leaf blades taste slightly peppery, while the ribs are sweet and juicy. Womboks can be used in coleslaw, sandwiches, casseroles, stir-fries and dumplings. The famous Korean relish, kim chi, is made from wombok pickled in salt, garlic and chilli.

Index of Recipes

Index of Recipes

About the Author

Spencer Clements
comes from a family
of fine cooks.

Spencer's mother and grandmother specialised in classical baking—beautiful cakes and pastries that left an impression on him as a young boy. In his early teens, Spencer worked at places such as The River, The Point, Lynchs, Fenix and Circa, and Taxi restaurant. He worked closely with the Mathis group running Chocolate Budda, and successfully opened Lower House at Melbourne's Federation Square. He then worked as a chef consultant to open Lamar's in South Melbourne for his close friends Michael and Victoria Lambie and Pam Lamar.

From this he developed a great love for modernising traditional recipes and he names Michael Lambie and Pierrre Kauffmann as his greatest influences.

These days, Spencer pursues his passion of gluten-free food through his website 'Edible for the Irritable' and conducts gluten-free cooking classes at several of Melbourne's leading technical and further educational institutions. Visit his website at www.efifoodstore.com.au.

Acknowledgements

There's always been something different going on in my day-to-day life as a chef. So I would like to say thanks to all those people that I've worked with as an apprentice chef and now a mature chef.

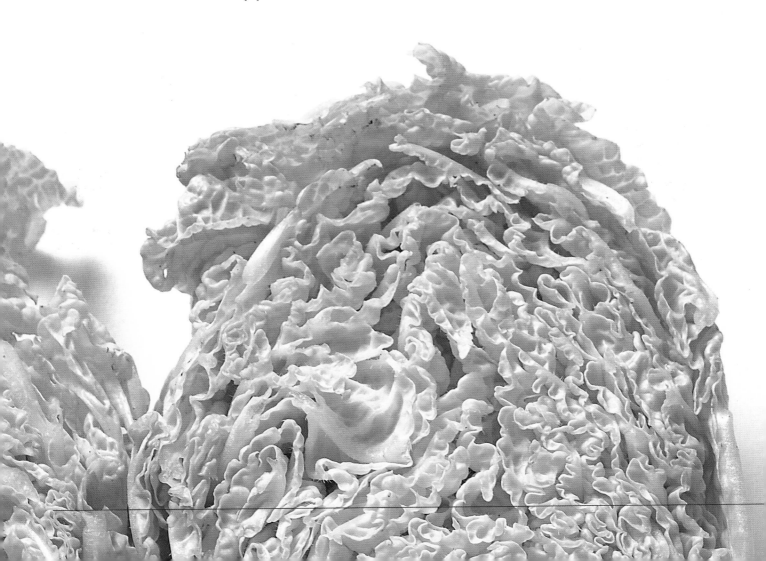

The major stepping-stone for me in my cooking career was restaurants, starting off with my cooking experience at Lynches. I'd like to say thanks to Old Lyncho, who was a very influential guide, and also to Chef Phillip Moore and long-time friend Greg Oshea.

Moving from Lynches, I got a real shock working at CIRCA at the Prince of Wales hotel. The chef owner Michael Lambi was, and still to this day, is my biggest mentor. Working for him in 1997, then again during 2002, working at Taxi, Chocolate Budda and opening Lower House, was a big wow for me. I then worked as a Chef Consultant, successfully re-opening Lamaros. Pam Lamaro, Michael and Victoria Lambi were fantastic and I would love to work with them anytime. Working with them has given me very good memories.

I can't forget the people who got me where I am today with my TV presenting and show presentations. Well, Gabriel Martin, you're it! If it wasn't for your kind heart, offering me your job while your wife was expecting twins, I wouldn't be doing any of this. My life has changed ten-fold, going from working with LG and the *Ready Steady Cook* road show, to doing live cooking demonstration at many shows in Melbourne, Sydney and Brisbane.

I fell in love with gluten-free food after being diagnosed with IBS and met a lady by the name of Sue Sheppard at the first gluten-free show in Melbourne. Through her guidance and help, she has pushed me along, making sure that I got recognised as much as possible, as has Jo Richardson, giving up her time while flying back and forth around the country. A big thanks to Sue and Jo!

In the first two years of being diagnosed with IBS, I had been thinking about ideas for a book and also a business. Now having my business set up, along came another angel. You wouldn't think being asked by some very close friends—Rachael and Cameron Horder—to be the Godparents would help me get a Book deal, but it did! What a way to meet Linda Williams, and thank goodness we did. You have been a very special support and so kind, thank you.

Last, but not least, I can't forget to thank my whole family, Mum and Dad, Tracy and Darren, Faye, John, Brett and Rosalind, Granddad and Nan up there in Heaven who has always inspired me to do my best and to do whatever makes me happy.

To my beautiful wife Shelley and my gorgeous children Chelsea, Bridget and Jordan, who have been through the brunt of everything, thank you, and I love you more.

To you, the public, I hope reading this book will give you something back, whether it's for you or for a friend in need, enjoy it and cherish it forever.

Spencer Clements

First published in Australia in 2010 by
New Holland Publishers (Australia) Pty Ltd
Sydney • Auckland • London • Cape Town

1/66 Gibbes Street Chatswood NSW 2067 Australia
218 Lake Road Northcote Auckland New Zealand
86 Edgware Road London W2 2EA United Kingdom
80 McKenzie Street Cape Town 8001 South Africa

National Library of Australia Cataloguing in Publication data
Clements, Spencer.

Edible for the irritable cookbook / Spencer Clements.

ISBN: 9781741109627 (pbk.)

Includes index.

Gluten-free diet--Recipes.
Cookery.
 641.56318

Publisher: Linda Williams
Publishing Manager: Lliane Clarke
Project Editor: Rochelle Fernandez
Designer: Donnah Dee Luttrell
Photographs: Graeme Gillies
Cover photograph: Graeme Gillies
Food stylist: Lee Blaylock
Production Manager: Olga Dementiev
Printer: Toppan Leefung Printing Ltd

10 9 8 7 6 5 4 3 2 1

Our thanks to: KitchenAid, Jo Richardson (Food Consultant, Peter McInnes, KitchenAid),
Alana Fletcher (Food Communications Manager, Peter McInnes, KitchenAid)